Wha

Dr. Rainer Mittelstaedt and hi. in this powerfully practical book you hold in your hand. Understanding how to mentor other leaders is a critical need in the Church today. Having known and worked with the Mittelstaedts for over twenty years, I have been able to observe his growing passion for this area of Christian leadership. He followed his passion with research and applied living. This book will become a must-have textbook for the future training of leaders who are being equipped for meaningful impact in their various spheres of ministry. It is practical and scripture-based, covering the why's as well as the how's in becoming an effective mentor. Every person who desires to follow the pattern of Christ in discipling for this generation and the next will treasure the insights found on these pages. Try it. It will change your life!

—Rev. Dr. Naomi Dowdy
Founder, Chancellor TCA College, Singapore
Former Senior Pastor, Trinity Christian Centre, Singapore
Trainer, Consultant, Mentor

Mentoring, as a subject, is much loved but often poorly defined, and imprecisely executed. *Ministering Forward* addresses this paradox by offering a simple, straightforward, and comprehensive approach for ministry mentoring relationships. More than just a step-by-step, how-to textbook—which clearly the book is—*Ministering Forward* offers a meaningful and convincing rationale for why leaders must embrace purposeful and competent mentoring to realize God-given vision and extend their impact beyond their lifetimes. If you want to build people, develop leaders, and transfer vision forward, but don't know where to start, reach for *Ministering Forward* first.

—Peter Dove
Southeast Asia Regional Director
Pentecostal Assemblies of Canada International Missions

It is an honour to endorse *Ministering Forward*, by Dr. Rainer Mittelstaedt. There are numerous high-quality resources available on the subject of coaching but few that do justice to providing clarity as to the why, what, how, when, where, who, and for whom of mentoring. This resource brings well-defined clarity to the question of why mentoring is so essential to multiply the growth, development, discipleship, and shaping of increasing numbers of high potential persons who will carry ministry forward.

Mittelstaedt's comparisons to other processes used for multiplication enhance the clarity of what the essence of mentoring is. The model depicting how mentoring is done brings functional clarity to the "how" of mentoring. The final section of the book provides guidance on how to keep mentoring clear, focused, and purposeful for team building and group work.

Having taught and actively engaged in coaching, mentoring, and facilitation for just under fifty years, this resource fills a resource gap that will be used as a guide for teaching and doing mentoring and coaching into the future. Thanks for an exceptional resource and I can't wait to add it to a course textbook list.

—Paul Magnus, PhD
President Emeritus, Distinguished Professor of Leadership
and Management with Briercrest and Tyndale Seminaries
Coach, Consultant, Facilitator

Born out of passionate curiosity, grounded in solid research, and animated by practical mentoring experience in a variety of cultural contexts, *Ministering Forward: Mentoring Tomorrow's Christian Leaders* is an indispensable tool for leaders who want to personally grow today and also leave a legacy for tomorrow through the lives they have engaged. Rainer Mittelstaedt has done a fantastic job in bringing the critical principle of mentoring alive in this work.

—Peter McIntosh
Lead Pastor, Bethel Pentecostal Church of Ottawa, Canada
Former Southeast Asia Regional Director, Pentecostal
Assemblies of Canada International Missions

Rainer and his wife Elizabeth are global workers with many years of experience doing exactly what this book talks about—making a strategic investment of their lives in mentoring leaders overseas. Rainer's work is solidly grounded in Scripture and rich in its depth of application, yet he writes in an easy-to-read style. This book comes from a person whose expertise is grounded in informed research as well as practical skills derived from actual engagement in the mentoring process. It thus represents a rare blend of robust scholarship and hands-on experience, covering an impressively broad spectrum of topics and material crucial to Christian leaders around the world. *Ministering Forward* addresses a great need in a much-neglected area in leadership training. If you are serious about being a mature leader who prepares other leaders for the Church of the future, then this book is for you!

—Dr. Ivan Satyavrata
Senior Pastor, Assembly of God Church in Kolkata
Chair, Board of World Vision-India
Chair, Bombay Teen Challenge
Author of *Holy Spirit, Lord and Life Giver*
and *God Has Not Left Himself Without Witness*
Former President, Southern Asia Bible College, Bangalore

It has been said that leaders don't lead followers, they lead other leaders. Rainer Mittelstaedt has captured the essence of this truth by not only providing a biblical and theoretical foundation for mentorship, but laying out a practical pathway for establishing mutually enriching leadership development relationships. Surely there is nothing more effective for producing godly leaders than living life-on-life with an emerging leader in an intentional mentorship experience. It is the ultimate leadership legacy.

—Dr. Kirk Kauffeldt
GlobalEd Director, Pentecostal Assemblies
of Canada International Missions

Mentoring is one of the tried and true methods of developing the next generation. Rainer has done the church—indeed, any leader—a service in providing not only the biblical rationale but practical and easily applicable ways to practice mentoring. Having worked in multiple cultural contexts, the author is sharing with us principles that will find relevance regardless of the context. I recommend the book highly.

—John F. Caplin
Certified Executive Coach

At a time when many talk about the need for personal work, discipling, and mentoring, but few are willing to devote the time to do such work, Rainer Mittelstaedt faithfully gives himself to investing in emerging leaders in Sri Lanka and elsewhere. This experience, combined with serious academic study on the topic, has resulted in a concise, comprehensive, and very practical book on mentoring. I pray that it would contribute to reversing the trend away from this vital ministry in the church.

—Dr. Ajith Fernando
Teaching Director, Youth for Christ Sri Lanka
Author, *Jesus Driven Ministry*

The empowering words and actions of a mentor always leave an indelible mark on the soul of their protégé. Living faith cannot be inherited; it must be passed on from one generation to another through the power of trusted mentorship. The cruelty of our critics will never erase the inspiration of our mentors. *Ministering Forward: Mentoring Tomorrow's Christian Leaders* exposes many theological and practical aspects of mentorship, in ways that are significantly relevant for every ministry context. This book is a must-read for every Christian leader and should be used as discipleship curriculum for local churches.

—Rev. Ken Russell
District Superintendent
Pentecostal Assemblies of Canada, BC and Yukon

Rainer's *Ministering Forward* is an exceptional manual on the important process of mentoring the next generation of Christian leaders in any cultural context of the world. The biblical accounts of leaders who invested in disciples and teams of servants provide solid practical examples for contemporary application. This book presents not only a wise rationale for mentoring but the core values and steps which must be taken to equip and enrich the next generation of productive leaders for the challenges we face today. I heartily recommend this book for those who are serious about discipleship and training.

—Dr. Wilf Hildebrandt
Dean of Education, Summit Pacific College

Ministering Forward is a biblically grounded, thorough, and accessible guide to practically walking alongside others in mentoring.

—Dr. Steve Brown
President, Arrow Leadership
Author of *Leading Me: Eight Practices for a Christian Leader's Most Important Assignment*

Leadership matters and the development [of] other leaders must be the life-long commitment of *all* leaders. At every point along the journey, leaders need mentors and models. Rainer Mittelstaedt offers a guide to those committed to multiplying godly influence through mentorship. This guide is rooted in the Scriptures and in the life of Jesus and has been tested in the multiple leadership contexts and cultures where Rainer has been a faithful witness for Christ. He has personally modeled the radical reversal from worldly leadership patterns, a reversal taught and modeled by Jesus and demanded of his followers. Enjoy these proven insights from a faithful servant of God.

—Rev. D. Murray Cornelius
Executive Director for International Missions
Pentecostal Assemblies of Canada

MINISTERING FORWARD

Mentoring Tomorrow's Christian Leaders

Merriam,

Be blessed as you invest in others

Rainer Mittelstaedt

RAINER MITTELSTAEDT

MINISTERING FORWARD
Copyright © 2017 by Rainer Mittelstaedt

All rights reserved. Neither this publication nor any part of this publication may be reproduced or transmitted in any form or by any means, electronic or mechanical, including photocopying, recording or any information storage and retrieval system, without permission in writing from the author.

Throughout the book, composite characters have been created for illustrative purposes. They are not intended to depict any one person's story.

Unless otherwise indicated, all scripture quotations are taken from the Holy Bible, NEW INTERNATIONAL VERSION®, NIV® Copyright © 1973, 1978, 1984, 2011 by Biblica, Inc.® Used by permission. All rights reserved worldwide. Scripture quotations marked ESV are from the ESV® Bible (The Holy Bible, English Standard Version®), copyright © 2001 by Crossway, a publishing ministry of Good News Publishers. Used by permission. All rights reserved.

Printed in Canada

ISBN: 978-1-4866-1500-1

Word Alive Press
131 Cordite Road, Winnipeg, MB R3W 1S1
www.wordalivepress.ca

Cataloguing in Publication may be obtained through Library and Archives Canada

To my wife Elizabeth,
for her loving encouragement, unwavering integrity, and deep faith.

And to our children, Marlies, Philip, and Richard,
who have been a source of much joy.

CONTENTS

FOREWORD	xv
INTRODUCTION	xvii
Purpose of the Book	xix
Overview of the Book	xxiii
Suggestions for Reading the Book	xxiv
Terminology	xxv

PART I: UNDERSTANDING MINISTRY MENTORING — 1

1. **WHAT IS MINISTRY MENTORING ANYWAY?** — 3
   - Defining Mentoring in General — 6
   - Christian Ministry Mentoring Defined — 8
   - The Distinctive Objectives of Ministry Mentoring — 13

2. **DIFFERENT PERSPECTIVES ON MENTORING** — 15
   - Developmental and Sponsorship Mentoring — 16
   - Formal and Informal Mentoring — 17
   - Peer Mentoring — 18
   - Reverse Mentoring — 18
   - Group Mentoring — 19
   - Effective and Ineffective Mentoring — 20
   - Formal Ministry Training and Ministry Mentoring — 21
   - A Christian Ministry Mentoring Model — 25

3. **MENTORING IN THE OLD TESTAMENT** — 29
   - In the Beginning, God… — 30
   - Moses and Mentoring — 33
   - Mentoring Relationships in the Old Testament — 36

4. HOW DID JESUS MENTOR? — 41
- Jesus as Mentor of the Apostles — 42
  - 1. Careful Selection — 43
  - 2. Intentional Association — 44
  - 3. Call to Commitment — 45
  - 4. Spiritual Impartation — 45
  - 5. Exemplary Demonstration — 46
  - 6. Delegation of Responsibilities — 46
  - 7. Supervision of Ministry — 47
  - 8. Expectation of Fruitfulness — 47
  - 9. Relational Growth — 48
  - 10. Personal Attention — 49
- The Holy Spirit as Mentor — 50

5. PAUL, THE SPIRITUAL PARENT MENTOR — 53
- Barnabas as Mentor — 54
- New Testament Mentoring Words — 55
- Paul as Mentor — 57
- Summarizing Biblical Mentoring Insights — 61

PART II: MINISTRY MENTORING IN PRACTICE — 63

6. WHAT MENTORS DO—MENTORING ACTIVITIES — 65
- Intentional Engagement—Selection of the Mentee — 66
- The Issue of Availability — 67
- Knowing the Mentee — 68
- Affirmation and Encouragement — 71
- The Potential Roles of a Mentor — 75

7. WHO MENTORS ARE—MENTORING ATTITUDE — 81
- What a Ministry Mentor Values — 81
- Embrace Your Mentoring Style — 83

	Maintain Your Relationship with God	85
	Self-awareness and Emotional Intelligence	85
	Self-care	86
	Productive and Competent	86
	Hold Yourself Accountable	87
	Humility	87
	Burden of Power and Idealization	88
	Intentional and Transparent Modeling	90
	Encourage Without Becoming Blind	93
	Do Not Expect Perfection	93
	Respect Privacy and Protect Confidentiality	94
	Use Humor	94
	Get Rid of Jealousy	94
	The Heart of a Mentor is Generous	95
8.	WHO THE MENTEE IS—MENTORING AWARENESS	97
	Toward a Mentoring Agenda	98
	Knowing the Story of the Mentee's Life	100
	Nudging the Mentee Toward Self-awareness	101
9.	HOW THE MENTEE LEARNS—THE MENTORING AGENDA	109
	Development of Character and Competency	109
	Determine the Mentoring Agenda	113
	Set the Learning Development Plan	115
	What is the Learning Style of the Mentee?	116
10.	BEING INTENTIONAL—THE MENTORING AGREEMENT	121
	The Nature of the Mentoring Relationship	122
	Beginning a Mentoring Relationship	125
	Setting Direction and Negotiating a Development Plan	129
	Concluding a Formal Mentoring Relationship	132
	Summary	133

11.	A WORD FOR THE MENTEE	135
	Why Do I Need a Mentor?	135
	What Happens in a Mentoring Relationship?	136
	How Can I Find the Right Mentor?	137
	How Can I Make the Most of a Mentoring Relationship?	139
12.	NAVIGATING CHALLENGES IN MINISTRY MENTORING	143
	Supervisory Relationships and Mentoring	143
	The Issue of Mixed Gender Mentorships	145
	The Issue of Power in a Mentoring Relationship	146
	Building Trust, Taking Risks	150
	When the Mentoring Relationship Breaks Down	152
	CONCLUSION	155
	Mentoring and Team Building	156
	Mentoring and Succession Planning	157
	Taking Steps Toward a Mentoring Culture	158
	One More Thing	161

APPENDIX A: MENTORING AGENDA PROCESS WORKSHEET	163
APPENDIX B: SAMPLE MENTORING AGREEMENT	165
APPENDIX C: COMPONENTS OF THE MINISTRY MENTORING MODEL EXPANDED	169
GLOSSARY	171
ACKNOWLEDGEMENTS	173
ABOUT THE AUTHOR	175
RECOMMENDED READING	177

FOREWORD

It is not very often that a mentee has the opportunity to gather on one stage at one time many of the mentors, both formal and informal, he has had in life. That was my opportunity in 2010 as one by one I told the story of how the fourteen people on the stage with me had shaped and influenced my spiritual life, character, and ministry competency. I also referred to several others who could not be there but had made meaningful contributions by mentoring me.

As I told their stories, I enumerated the principles they had modelled that are crucial to mentoring and disciple-making. Character, accessibility, correction, wisdom, intentionality, resourcing, spiritual maturity, selflessness, empowerment, and so much more had been offered to me through their lives. And I had responded with respect, availability, a desire to learn, and a willingness to apply what I had learned. Through these relational practices, qualities had been developed in my life that are still being developed today.

My friend and colleague Rainer Mittelstaedt, in *Ministering Forward: Mentoring Tomorrow's Christian Leaders*, takes the theology, attitudes, and practices of mentoring within a Christian leadership context and in a comprehensive and practical manner provides valuable insights for mentors or mentees.

Drawing from his own life experience and an extensive knowledge of classic and recent literature on the subject, Rainer provides a systematic overview of mentoring within Scripture. The opportunity to review the biblical principles of mentoring, especially from Jesus' ministry of disciple-making in the gospels, is inspiring and informative.

What follows will prove to be as valuable as gold for those who want to take their mentoring ministry to a higher level. Rainer offers intentional, highly practical wisdom and methods for mentors and mentees. He comprehensively guides leaders through the mentoring relationship, including the nature of their relationship, the skillsets and attitudes needed, and the practical processes to be followed. Practical resources are provided to assist with follow through.

I am sure it will become clear to you, as it is to me, that the way Rainer addresses this subject goes well beyond the theoretical. He has benefited from the mentors who have poured into his life and he has intentionally mentored others in life and ministry. Some have become his successors who continue to serve with excellence. I am grateful that through *Ministering Forward: Mentoring Tomorrow's Christian Leaders* we can all benefit from this man's passion to see people mentored well.

—Rev. Dr. David R. Wells
General Superintendent, The Pentecostal Assemblies of Canada
June 2017

INTRODUCTION

During my teen years, I helped my father build cabins at a Christian camp. Dad was the pastor of a small church, but he was also a carpenter who used his skills to supplement the family income. He took me along with him to help.

I enjoyed these times because it gave me the opportunity to spend quality time with Dad in an otherwise very busy phase of his life. One of the first things he taught me was how to hammer nails without damaging the wood. At the time, I thought I was helping him, but I soon realized he could have finished the job much more quickly had he done it himself. It was much later that I understood these trips to the camp hadn't been just about me helping him build cabins; they had been about me spending time with Dad and developing a relationship with him. I learned many life lessons during our lunchtime discussions, and I observed how he related to other workers.

He was more than just my father; he was also my mentor. We didn't use that term in those days, but what we now call mentoring indeed happened in our relationship. And yes, I did acquire some basic carpentry skills.

Years later, when I entered the ministry, my father became my ministry mentor. It was not a formal, spelled-out arrangement, but we served together. I worked with him as his assistant pastor. He had experience. I was inexperienced. I watched him do ministry, and we talked about it. He watched me do ministry and provided feedback. He knew how to do this mentoring thing because that's what they do in the construction industry, except they call it "apprenticeship."

We only worked together for a few months, but this season became the basis of many mentoring encounters with him in a lifetime of ministry. Since then, I've had many other mentors who have enriched my life and ministry. I have also had the opportunity to relate to others in a mentoring role.

At one point, a younger minister was assigned to me so I could supervise and advise him in his ministerial duties and activities. We agreed on some ground rules for the relationship and set a fixed weekly time to meet. We also had other opportunities to meet from time to time in a variety of ministry contexts. I established an open-door policy in which he usually had access to me. We had what I would now call an "intentional ministry mentoring relationship."

My focus in this relationship was twofold: what was God's best for this young minister, and how could I help the kingdom of God advance through his ministry? His focus was to receive the benefit of my life and ministry experience and apply it to his life and ministry.

As we met on a regular basis, we dealt with character issues, family matters, ministry strategies, ministry competencies, and relationships with other people—essentially no subject was off-limits. I would encourage, advise, and challenge. He would share his heart, his dreams, and his concerns. This mentoring context became a safe place for him to test his theories and ideas about life and ministry. I was a sounding board.

For the most part, I resisted telling him what I thought he should do, but I gave him the benefit of my opinions on ministry practices and relational issues, for whatever they were worth. This arrangement, which we kept in place for several years, contributed to a fruitful ministry for the younger minister. I was also thoroughly enriched as I gleaned from his perspective and participated in his excitement when things were going well, and his disappointments when there were setbacks.

Thinking back on this scenario, I was grateful for the privilege of having had the opportunity to make a positive impact on him, as well as having received the blessings of sharing in another's ministry. I have subsequently had opportunities to mentor others in a variety of ministry contexts, with both positive and negative experiences and outcomes.

On further reflection, I realized that I could be a mentor because I had been the beneficiary of mentors at different times throughout my own ministry journey. Others had invested time and demonstrated care for my development. I had also experienced times of looking for and not finding mentors who would walk with me during some of the crucial phases of ministry. There were also times when I wasn't the best mentor to those who may have been looking for it from me. Sometimes I just didn't know how to do it given the circumstance. Other times I didn't have or make the time.

The combination of these experiences motivated me to understand better what mentoring is and how it works. This curiosity led me to research the subject in the context of a Doctor of Ministry project. Together with the ministry leaders who participated in the project, we learned some of the things you will be reading about here. I have since had the opportunity to teach seminars and courses in several other contexts.

The insights gained in the thesis project, and further interaction with seminar participants, students, and ongoing mentoring relationships, are incorporated here. I have included a few sections of the thesis in this book.[1] These have been adapted and updated to fit the style and content of the book. However, most of the book is new writing which flows out of the fundamental insights gained in the study, but it also represents additional insights gained from further experience, study, and reflection.

PURPOSE OF THE BOOK

Many good books and articles about mentoring exist from a variety of perspectives, and I have received benefit from the ones I have had the opportunity to read and study. I nonetheless felt compelled to write this book to provide an opportunity for men and women in all kinds of ministry contexts to better understand what mentoring is and invite them to integrate mentoring into their ministry. This book views mentoring through a biblical lens but demonstrates awareness of mentoring principles and

---

1 Rainer Eugene Mittelstaedt, "The Development and Implementation of a Ministry Mentoring Model in a Sri Lankan Context" (DMin Thesis, Tyndale University College and Seminary, 2013).

practices from many backgrounds. It also outlines a process which leads to purposeful mentoring relationships from start to finish.

The primary purpose of this book is to describe the practice of mentoring in a way that will help mentors to become more skilled as they relate to their mentees. The desired outcome is that mentees will more readily receive what their mentors can provide for them. The focus is on Christian ministry mentoring, but many of the same principles presented here can also apply to mentoring in general.

There are those who intuitively mentor well because they have experienced good mentoring or because they naturally have a generous attitude toward those around them. Those who are predisposed toward mentoring others in this way may already be exemplifying many of the principles this book describes. They may even wonder why a book such as this one is necessary. Others may find themselves in a mentoring relationship and are looking for some ideas to help them be better mentors.

I have also observed that many seek the guidance of good mentors but don't find mentors who can provide what they need. They find themselves in ministry contexts where they aren't encouraged to grow. Those in leadership who could provide guidance don't see mentoring as part of their ministry. The result is that emerging leaders have left those ministry settings to seek out situations where more mentoring support is available. Some even launch out on their own to start independent ministries. I can think of some who are successful partly because they found supportive mentors who weren't threatened by the mentee's success. But I am also aware of others where the outcome was not as positive.

It is my hope that this book helps raise awareness about mentoring and highlights effective ministry mentoring. I'd like to encourage people at every level of ministry to consider how they can be mentors for those who are less experienced in ministry but are willing learners. Perhaps this book can play a part in drawing more leaders into mentoring engagements. I am confident that the book can also be a resource to help those already mentoring to improve their mentoring skills.

The underlying philosophy of ministry which gives the impetus for mentoring flows out of this passage of Scripture:

> *When he saw the crowds, he had compassion on them, because they were harassed and helpless, like sheep without a shepherd. Then he said to his disciples, "The harvest is plentiful but the workers are few. Ask the Lord of the harvest, therefore, to send out workers into his harvest field."*
>
> *Jesus called his twelve disciples to him and gave them authority to drive out impure spirits and to heal every disease and sickness.*
>
> —Matthew 9:36–10:1[2]

Jesus had a deep compassion for people. He observed that they were like sheep without a shepherd. His response was a call to pray for workers, followed by the calling and empowering of the apostles to minister to the people. As we will see in Chapter Four, the training of these apostles was an integral part of his mission so that people would enjoy the leadership and care of good shepherds.

To underline this, the Gospel of John includes the story of Jesus' post-resurrection encounter with the apostle Peter. Jesus responds to Peter's threefold affirmation of love for his Lord with these directives: *"Feed my lambs"* (John 21:15), *"Take care of my sheep"* (John 21:16), and *"Feed my sheep"* (John 21:17). This experience was undoubtedly in Peter's mind many years later when he penned these words:

> *Be shepherds of God's flock that is under your care, watching over them— not because you must, but because you are willing, as God wants you to be; not pursuing dishonest gain, but eager to serve; not lording it over those entrusted to you, but being examples to the flock. And when the Chief Shepherd appears, you will receive the crown of glory that will never fade away.*
>
> —1 Peter 5:2–4

For the church to have an abundance of Christian ministers who embrace those words, we must be intentional in developing Christian leaders at every level who will be good shepherds for the sake of the people of God, his flock.

---

2   *"He appointed twelve that they might be with him and that he might send them out to preach"* (Mark 3:14).

Christian leadership development entails more than attaining competence, accumulating knowledge, and learning the mechanics of leading people. It is also about growing in character and developing spiritual and emotional maturity. If Christian leaders fail to pay attention to their spiritual growth while at the same time increasing their ministry skills, we cannot expect the church to advance. However, if we have good leaders, we will have healthy churches. If we have healthy churches, we will have healthy sheep. If we have healthy sheep, they will multiply, and the *"gospel of the kingdom will be preached in the whole world as a testimony to all nations"* (Matthew 24:14).

A major premise of this book is that intentional ministry mentoring done well needs to be part of any program of Christian leadership development. Mentoring relationships will enhance the preparation of those entering the ministry and produce leaders of vibrant faith and dedicated service to God. I believe there is a shortage of good ministry mentors. Except for a few cases where a culture of mentoring exists in local churches, or where individuals have embraced mentoring as part of their ministry, there is a gap in many places around the world that needs to be filled. This can be addressed by challenging leaders to integrate mentoring into their ministry schedules and train them how to be excellent mentors. The research suggests that those who have good mentoring experiences have a greater chance at being successful in their vocations. This holds true in the Christian ministry as well. For instance, J. Robert Clinton, who has studied the lives of Christian leaders for many years, writes in *The Making of a Leader*:

> Comparative study of many leaders' lives indicates the frequency with which other people were significant in challenging them into leadership and in giving timely advice and help so as to keep them there. Leaders who are effective and finish well will have from ten to fifteen significant people who came alongside at one time or another to help them.[3]

---

3   J. Robert Clinton, *The Making of a Leader: Recognizing the Lessons and Stages of Leadership Development*, revised edition (Colorado Springs, CO: NavPress, 2012), 214. Clinton has studied the lives of over 1,300 leaders.

Where such mentoring is lacking, those in ministry are less than they could be and the advance of the gospel of the kingdom is delayed.

Excellent mentors are competent in their work. They continually grow in character and knowledge. They show consistent interest in the development of their mentees. They give of their time and make themselves available to their mentees. They also work at improving their mentoring skills. These qualities may seem a bit overwhelming, but as we will see, mentors do not have to be perfect; they must simply have a passion for helping advance the next generation of ministers, and they must be willing to invest their time in them intentionally.

OVERVIEW OF THE BOOK

The first part of the book helps us to understand ministry mentoring. I explain the "what" and "why" of mentoring. This is the theoretical part of the book. Chapter One gives a definition of ministry mentoring as it is used in this book and describes it in comparison to other formational learning activities. In Chapter Two, we look at mentoring from different perspectives and consider a model of ministry mentoring. In the next three chapters, I highlight mentoring examples in Scripture and discuss how these provide a biblical foundation and rationale for how we can mentor today. Chapter Three focuses on Old Testament examples and insights concerning mentoring, beginning with a theological reflection on God as the original mentor. In Chapter Four, we look at how Jesus mentored his disciples and how his mentoring ministry continues through the Holy Spirit. In Chapter Five, we highlight some New Testament keywords that relate to mentoring. We also discuss the benevolent parent mentoring model we find in the ministry of the Apostle Paul.

The second part of the book describes the practice of ministry mentoring, in which I explain the "how," "who," and "for whom" of mentoring. This part contains the more practical aspects of mentoring. Chapter Six begins by describing several mentoring activities and skills that need to be added to the toolbox of a ministry mentor. It also includes a repertoire of roles that mentors might play as they interact with their mentees. Chapter

Seven follows by speaking of the person and attitude of a good mentor. The focus is on the heart and characteristics of a mentor. Chapter Eight deals with developing an awareness of who the mentee is by helping the mentor understand their story and where they are in their spiritual journey. Chapter Nine builds on that to show how to set the mentoring agenda, which is about the learning objectives, critical growth pathways, and development plans the mentor negotiates with the mentee. The mentoring agenda defines the core of the mentee's learning. Chapter Ten describes how a mentoring agreement can be structured. The agreement is an important part of what makes a mentoring relationship intentional. Chapter Eleven specifically addresses potential mentees. Mentors should also read this chapter and then make it available to their mentees and those who seek mentors. Chapter Twelve helps to navigate some of the challenges in ministry mentoring. The conclusion suggests some of the broader applications of mentoring relationships.

SUGGESTIONS FOR READING THE BOOK

I like to read a book from beginning to end in the order it was written. But I recognize that not everyone learns that way and it is not the only way to read a book such as this. So you may decide to work your way through the chapters following another order. That is fine. However, I suggest that after you read the introduction, at least read Chapter One before you read other chapters, because it provides the working definition of ministry mentoring that is used throughout the book. After that, you will be able to dive into whichever chapter interests you the most and follow your own reading plan.

For instance, if you are more interested in how mentoring works, you may want to get into Chapter Six on mentoring activities earlier than later. But do take time to read Chapter Seven on the mentoring attitude which follows, because it is closely connected.

If you are more interested in a mentee's perspective, you can go directly to Chapter Eleven. If you want to understand how to determine what the mentee should focus on in a mentoring relationship, go to Chapters

Eight and Nine, where the mentoring agenda is explained. These two chapters also belong together.

If you want to learn how to set up a mentoring relationship, study Chapter Ten on the mentoring agreement.

If you want to study how Jesus mentored, go to Chapter Four. The apostle Paul's mentoring model is described in Chapter Five. If you haven't yet read about mentoring in the Old Testament, you will be blessed by some of the insights gained from the mentoring stories highlighted in Chapter Three. Don't forget to read Chapter Two, because there you will see how the ministry mentoring model in this book fits together and how it relates to other kinds of mentoring.

It is my prayer that as you read this book,

- you will be inspired to mentor someone,
- you will gain additional mentoring skills to guide mentees toward effective ministry for the sake of the kingdom of God,
- you will understand what it takes to have an intentional mentoring relationship,
- you will take the steps that lead to an intentional mentoring relationship, and
- you will become a member of the growing tribe who integrates a culture of ministry mentoring into their contexts.

TERMINOLOGY

Many of the terms in the book will be familiar to those who work in church contexts, parachurch organizations, or Christian ministries. As I write about Christian ministry mentoring, I have all of these in view, even though I may use the terms "church," "organization," or "ministry context" interchangeably. When I speak of mentors, mentees, ministers, and leaders, I consider both men and women. This is reflected by interchanging the pronouns "he" and "she" or "him" and "her" at various points in the descriptions. Sometimes I may use phrases like "he or she" and "him or her" to indicate gender inclusivity. Sometimes I use "their" and "they" for that same purpose.

But I also want to explain how I use the word "ministry," since it may not be obvious to everyone. Ministry and service mean the same thing. However, the word ministry in Christian circles has taken on a vocational nuance. God calls some to serve him in full-time ministry, and others God calls to serve him in part-time ministry. Part-time ministers are often bi-vocational in that they supplement their income through another vocation. Lay ministers are called to serve God on a volunteer basis. Serving God includes serving his people in the church and those outside the church. Ideally, as Christians, we are all to be involved in ministry and participate in the Great Commission (Matthew 28:19–20). Thus, the prospect of mentoring men and women for ministry does not just apply to those in "professional" or paid ministry. It includes all who may serve the Lord in any capacity and might benefit from a ministry mentoring relationship.

We have been saved to serve, but we serve according to the calling and gifting God has given to each one. This means that each one has a different function in ministry.

> *Each of you should use whatever gift you have received to serve others, as faithful stewards of God's grace in its various forms. If anyone speaks, they should do so as one who speaks the very words of God. If anyone serves, they should do so with the strength God provides, so that in all things God may be praised through Jesus Christ. To him be the glory and the power for ever and ever. Amen.*
> —1 Peter 4:10–11

Other terms which are unique to the subject matter of the book will usually be defined as they appear, or they will be understood by context. You will also find explanations of some terms in the glossary at end of the book.

Part I

UNDERSTANDING MINISTRY MENTORING

Chapter One

WHAT IS MINISTRY MENTORING ANYWAY?

MENTORING IS AN IMPORTANT MINISTRY TOOL THAT WILL ENABLE YOU TO multiply your ministry beyond your own lifetime. Undoubtedly, God has given you a vision and mission for your ministry. Only God knows if you will be able to accomplish that mission in your lifetime. In any case, you will not be able to do it alone. Consider these biblical examples:

- God gave Moses a vision to rescue the people of Israel from Egyptian slavery and establish them in the Promised Land.
- King David had a dream of building a great temple in Jerusalem to the glory of God.
- Jesus came on a mission to establish a kingdom on earth where peace and righteousness would rule.
- Paul had a vision to take the gospel to the ends of the earth.

What each of these people has in common is that none of them accomplished their vision or dream in their lifetime. However, the mission was eventually accomplished, or is on its way to being accomplished. They themselves did not finish what they began, but it was destined to be fulfilled because it was a part of God's plan and design. How? Moses had his Joshua; David, his Solomon; Jesus, his apostles; and Paul, his Timothy, Titus, and others. A key part of their success was that they taught, trained, and equipped those who followed them. They mentored others to share in the vision. The Spirit of God provided for the continuity of the mission and their followers carried it forward.

Most people have experienced the help and advice of others who have preceded them in their career or ministry. In mentorship training sessions, I often ask participants to identify three people in their life who have helped get them where they are today. People cite a boss, a pastor, parents, or other significant individuals who have influenced them and encouraged them in their life, career, or ministry journey. They sometimes refer to this kind of help as "mentoring," and those who provide it as "mentors." Thus, as we approach this subject, I assume that most people have participated both in the giving and receiving of mentoring in one form or another even if they may have used other terms to describe it.

One of the first books on mentoring from a Christian perspective is Ted Engstrom's *The Fine Art of Mentoring*. Gordon MacDonald, in the foreword, suggests that mentoring was not written about in earlier times because it was an accepted part of life.

> In contrast to the past, the mentoring function today is in short supply… Today what passes for people development happens in a classroom, and the certification of a person is by diploma from an institution rather than the stamp of approval from an overseer, a mentor.[4]

Mentoring, as a practice, has been a part of human experience throughout history, though it has not necessarily gone by that name. James M. Houston, in *The Disciple*, writes,

> Mentors have been around perhaps as long as the human race. Shamans and witch doctors, prophets and philosophers, leaders and teachers go back deep into our history. Moses and Joshua, Confucius and Mencius, Socrates and Plato, Hillel and the

---

4   Theodore Wilhelm Engstrom and Norman B. Rohrer, *The Fine Art of Mentoring: Passing on to Others What God Has Given You*, first edition (Brentwood, TN: Wolgemuth & Hyatt, 1989), x.

Pharisees, have all transmitted their ways of life from teacher to pupil, mentor to mentee. Thus, the minds of great thinkers have been passed from generation to generation. Their efficacy as teachers also has been in being exemplars, providing a way of life that could be imitated in deed as well as thought.[5]

There has been an increased interest in mentoring in the last thirty years or so. Houston explains four reasons for this renewed search for mentors in our time, which I summarize here:

1. We are disenchanted by disembodied generalizations and long for those who model truth.
2. We are recognizing the need to engage wise friends in learning relationships rather than simply looking for "fixers" or "teachers" of instrumental knowledge.
3. We are awakening to the need of mentors as we observe and experience the increasing isolation of individuals in a society that lacks in honest feedback.
4. We are looking for those "who live as they talk, who integrate theory with practice."[6]

This renewed interest also relates partly to a growing sense that formal institutional educational models do not by themselves address the needs of learners for the practical realities of life and work.

When we talk about mentoring, we usually think about someone less experienced who is being helped by someone more experienced. There are many possible scenarios in which this can happen: a one-time informal mentoring activity or encounter, a lifelong informal mentoring relationship, an intentional short-term relationship guided by a mentoring agreement, or a structured mentoring program within an organization or institution.

---

5 James M. Houston, *The Disciple: Following the True Mentor*, volume five, Soul's Longing Series (Colorado Springs, CO: David C. Cook, 2007), 23.
6 Ibid., 24–5.

I believe it is helpful to distinguish between *mentoring activities* and *mentoring relationships*. Most people have experienced various kinds of mentoring activities as spontaneous occurrences throughout their lives. Fewer people have experienced the intentional and ongoing learning relationships between a mentor and a mentee. This book will describe mentoring activities within the context of mentoring relationships. The objective is to promote an increase in effective Christian ministry mentorships.

DEFINING MENTORING IN GENERAL

The term "mentor" was first introduced into modern usage by François Fénelon's *Les Aventures de Telemaque*, written in 1699. This book retells Homer's epic poem *The Odyssey*, in which Odysseus appointed his servant, Mentor, to take care of his son while he was away fighting the Trojan War. Andy Roberts, in a literary analysis, has demonstrated that "it is Fenelon, not Homer, who endows his Mentor with the qualities, abilities, and attributes that have come to be incorporated into the action of modern day mentoring."[7]

Eventually, the word "mentor" was used to refer to one who was at the same time a trusted advisor, teacher, and wise person.

Mentors are typically the benefactors in mentoring relationships in that they make their accrued knowledge, skills, wisdom, and experience available to their mentees. They are learning guides for mentees who acknowledge the need for this kind of support in their journey of personal and vocational development. The role of the mentor is analogous to that of a teacher, parent, guardian, advisor, counsellor, tutor, or someone in a similar position. While the functions they fulfill are helpful to consider in describing a mentor, for clarity we will define a mentor as a guide who agrees to be in a learning relationship with a mentee which primarily focuses on the personal and vocational development of the mentee.

In a mentoring relationship, the person being mentored is variously referred to as the mentee, mentoree, apprentice, disciple, intern, student, learner, novice, and more formally the protégé. This book will primarily

---

[7] Andy Roberts, "Homer's Mentor: Duties Fulfilled or Misconstrued." November 1999 (http://www.nickols.us/homers_mentor.pdf).

use the word "mentee" to refer to the person being mentored. When I quote other authors on the subject, I will retain their label.

Before we look at this book's definition of mentoring, let's take a glance at a sample of definitions. For instance, Johnson and Ridley researched mentoring in various professions and collaborated in the writing of *The Elements of Mentoring*. They give us a general contemporary definition:

> Mentoring relationships (mentorships) are dynamic, reciprocal, personal relationships in which a more experienced person (mentor) acts as a guide, role model, teacher, and sponsor of a less experienced person (protégé).[8]

Smither, in *Augustine as Mentor*, proposes another general definition:

> Though the contexts and the cultures may vary, mentoring, in essence, means that a master, expert, or someone with significant experience is imparting knowledge and skill to a novice in an atmosphere of discipline, commitment, and accountability.[9]

In their book *Connecting*, Stanley and Clinton provide a definition from a Christian perspective:

> Mentoring is a relational experience through which one person empowers another by sharing God-given resources.[10]

---

8   W. Brad Johnson and Charles R. Ridley, *The Elements of Mentoring*, revised edition (New York, NY: Palgrave Macmillan, 2008), xi.
9   Edward L. Smither, *Augustine as Mentor: A Model for Preparing Spiritual Leaders*, Kindle edition (Nashville, TN: B & H Academic, 2008), 4.
10 Paul D. Stanley and J. Robert Clinton, *Connecting: The Mentoring Relationships You Need to Succeed in Life* (Colorado Springs, CO: NavPress, 1992), 12. They also give an expanded definition: "Mentoring is a relational process, in which a mentor who knows or has experienced something, transfers that something (resources of wisdom, information, experience, confidence, insight, relationships, status, etc.) to a mentoree, at an appropriate time and manner, so that it facilitates development or empowerment" (40).

This is how Engstrom explains it:

> Mentoring is much more expansive than simply teaching and/or training. It is investing time and prayer. It is building relationships and investing emotionally in the transfer of values and skills and attitudes. Discipling talks about discipline, while mentoring talks about relationship.[11]

In this book, we define mentoring as a formational learning activity in the context of a relationship built on mutual trust by which the mentor guides the development of the mentee along critical growth pathways in life and vocation. Vocation here refers to a career, profession, calling, or sense of destiny about the mentee's life's work.

CHRISTIAN MINISTRY MENTORING DEFINED

As mentioned, our focus will be on Christian ministry mentoring, so let us look at the full definition we are using for the purposes of this book: *Christian ministry mentoring is a formational learning activity in the context of a relationship built on mutual trust by which the mentor guides the spiritual growth and ministry development of the mentee in cooperation with the Holy Spirit along critical growth pathways toward Christian maturity, ministry wisdom, and discernment for ministry engagement.*

We will describe this expanded definition in detail under various headings. Each heading points to an aspect of mentoring.

A Formational Learning Activity (Among Others)

There are any number of formational learning activities that are used to facilitate the development of adult learners. Descriptions and attempts to define these different learning activities sometimes overlap. For instance, mentoring is sometimes confused with coaching. To differentiate between the two, we can say that coaching tends to be more focused on

---

11 Engstrom and Rohrer, 73.

specific behaviours or skills whereas "mentoring often addresses or focuses on issues that are broader than those covered in the typical coaching relationship."[12]

Coaching conversations are nonetheless among the tools that a mentor frequently uses when engaging the mentee. It is also possible that some coaching engagements become very much like mentoring relationships as they expand into other areas of life and vocation of the person being coached or mentored. Another difference is that a formal coaching arrangement often involves financial payment for coaching sessions and the person being coached is considered a client. In contrast, mentoring arrangements tend to be volunteer agreements. In organizational settings, job descriptions often include mentoring as part of ongoing internal employee development programs.

At various times in the mentoring engagement, the mentor adds other formational learning activities as needed. These may include teaching, training, counselling, and consulting, but by themselves they are not the same as mentoring.

To come at it from the opposite perspective, we can also say that teachers, counsellors, and consultants from time to time move beyond their primary activities and become mentors to the people they engage. Figure 1 illustrates how mentoring relates to other formational learning disciplines and activities.

When it comes to spiritual character development or spiritual formation, Christian ministry mentoring also includes discipleship. Especially in the early stages, such a mentoring relationship will seem like basic discipleship in that it addresses many of the same issues of spiritual development. We will discuss this aspect of ministry mentoring in detail in Chapter Eight.

Discipleship often refers to the spiritual formation of a newly converted person until they mature. However, ministry mentoring from the outset pays attention to leadership development and ministry competencies in a way that discipleship may not necessarily address. Another formational

---

12   Tammy D. Allen, Lisa M. Finkelstein, and Mark L. Poteet, *Designing Workplace Mentoring Programs: An Evidence-Based Approach*, Talent Management Essentials (Malden, MA: Wiley-Blackwell, 2009), 3.

learning activity in the field of spiritual formation is spiritual direction. In this relationship, a spiritual director helps an individual discern the movements of the Holy Spirit in his or her life. This kind of spiritual mentoring is also a part of what transpires in a ministry mentoring relationship.

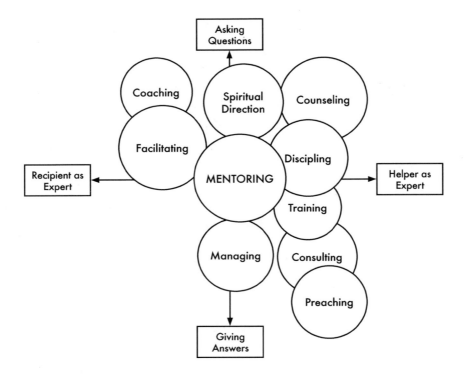

Figure 1: Mentoring and Other Formational Learning Activities[13]

In the day-to-day practice of mentoring as a formational learning activity, it is not usually necessary to distinguish between these different activities. One kind of mentoring activity flows seamlessly into another according to the needs of the situation. However, being aware of these activities enables the mentor to improve his or her mentoring skills in the different kinds of mentoring activities. In Chapter Six we will look in more detail at

---

13   I have adapted the concept of this diagram from Stephen G. Fairley and Chris E. Stout, *Getting Started in Personal and Executive Coaching: How to Create a Thriving Coaching Practice* (Hoboken, NJ: J. Wiley & Sons, 2004), 30.

the various formational learning activities relating to mentoring when we discuss the different roles a mentor may play in the mentoring relationship.

A Relationship Built on Mutual Trust

According to our definition, for a mentoring relationship to qualify as such, it requires that both the mentor and the mentee be aware of the relationship, even if they do not explicitly call it a mentoring relationship. A mentoring relationship is *reciprocal*, which means that there is an ongoing interaction between the mentor and the mentee. In this relationship, the mentor is willing to mentor the mentee, and the mentee wants to be mentored by the mentor. There is an agreement of some kind which determines the level of formality of the relationship. They trust one another in the areas of mentoring focus, and usually in other spheres of life and work as well. They agree on expectations, which provide for learning accountability in the relationship. There is a clear understanding of confidentiality about sensitive matters. It usually also involves sharing with one another on various issues of life experience. This relationship is, in fact, a kind of friendship that has the potential to deepen as time passes. We will look at some of these aspects of the mentoring relationship in Chapters Six and Seven.

Sometimes people identify authors and historical people who have influenced them as their mentors.[14] These connections are not real mentorships since the relationship is not *reciprocal*. A more accurate label is *self-directed learning*. This clarification of terms in no way minimizes the great modelling and teaching roles that these authors and historical people play in a person's overall development journey. In fact, a mentor may point a mentee to their heroes of the past as examples and suggest books and resources of authors that will enhance the learning of the mentee.

My mother is an avid reader of good spiritual books, and in her mentoring role over the years she has put life-changing books into my hands that have impacted my spiritual journey and ministry. One of the first authors to whom she introduced me was Watchman Nee, a Chinese pastor who had

---

14   For instance, Stanley and Clinton, 131–55, call it passive mentoring and describe the contemporary mentor who is still living but is not in a direct relationship with the mentee, and the historical mentor who has passed away. The mentee is influenced by them through other means such as video, audio, autobiographical writing and books.

an international influence through his writings. I never had a conversation with him, but his books sure made an impression on me. I can't say he was my mentor, because he didn't know who I was. In this case, my mother was the mentor with whom I could process what I learned in my reading.

The Mentor Guides the Development of the Mentee

In a mentoring relationship, the mentee takes ownership of his or her learning and development. Mentees express their learning needs as they understand them and show an interest in learning. The mentor, as the more knowledgeable and experienced person, primarily guides the learning experience. At the beginning of the relationship, the mentor may need to provide a little more direction concerning the areas of focus. But as the relationship develops and the mentee matures, the mentee is in a better position to determine his or her learning needs. This concept is developed throughout Chapters Six through Ten.

Cooperation with the Holy Spirit

As the human agent in the mentoring engagement, the ministry mentor is sensitive to the Holy Spirit's activity in the life of the mentee. Since the Holy Spirit is the divine mentor of the mentee, the mentor guides the mentee while continually asking the question, "What is God doing in the life of the mentee and how am I to facilitate that?" The mentor also pays attention to the broader concerns of the kingdom of God in the ministry context of the mentee. Thinking of it in this way helps the mentor remain aware of the human-divine partnership that is in play throughout the mentorship.

Critical Growth Pathways

Each mentee has unique learning needs based on their life and ministry journey, learning style, and current ministry context. The mentor and mentee need to determine the mentoring agenda and what the critical growth pathways might be. Critical growth pathways refer to the means by which the mentee moves toward fulfilling the learning objectives. The mentee, as the driver of this relationship, has learning needs that relate to the immediate ministry context. The mentor assists the mentee to map out the critical growth pathways toward the learning that needs to occur. The mentor may from time to time point out additional areas of concern for learning and development.

We will consider critical growth pathways in more depth in Chapters Eight and Nine, where I discuss the mentoring agenda of an intentional mentoring relationship.

THE DISTINCTIVE OBJECTIVES OF MINISTRY MENTORING

In a mentoring relationship, all areas are potentially open for discussion—life issues as well as ministry matters. How the mentee works toward rightly relating to all of life and ministry in a healthy and functional way is the guiding question. Ministry mentoring considers the impact of a mentee on the people in the ministry context, as it involves the ministry team and the people who receive ministry.

Christian ministry mentoring has as its focus the development of ministry leaders. Ministers are those who are involved in or are aspiring to be active in various leadership roles in church or parachurch ministries, including those having apostolic, prophetic, evangelistic, pastoral, and teaching ministries as well as those involved in administration and serving (Ephesians 4:11 and Romans 12:6–8). Christian ministry mentoring, however, is not limited to those aspiring to higher leadership positions. It can also be used as a training method for people who aspire to serve at any level of ministry. The principles are the same.

Ministry mentoring focuses on the development of Christian character in the minister and seeks a high standard of Christian maturity. Consider, for instance, this scripture: *"Not many of you should become teachers, my fellow believers, because you know that we who teach will be judged more strictly"* (James 3:1). Ministry mentoring is also concerned with ministry skills and leadership competencies that are required in Christian ministry contexts. The mentor engages the mentee concerning her unique ministry calling, helping the mentee navigate her ministry journey toward appropriate placement in ministry according to her natural ability, acquired skills, and spiritual gifts.

In the next chapter, we will look at different kinds of mentoring and provide a synopsis of the Christian mentoring model that forms the framework of this book.

QUESTIONS: FROM REFLECTION TO ACTION

1. What vision and mission do you have that you would like to be able to project beyond your lifetime? How do you think you could do that?
2. Who has helped you get to where you are today in ministry?
3. What kinds of relationships are you currently in that may fit into the definition of a mentoring relationship as described in this chapter? Are you a mentee or a mentor?
4. Can you identify some people in your ministry context who would benefit from a mentoring relationship? How would it help them? How do you see yourself engaging them?

Chapter Two

DIFFERENT PERSPECTIVES ON MENTORING

As we seek to understand what ministry mentoring is, we can learn much from those who have researched mentoring in other fields. Some who have dug deeper into the subject observe that "mentoring is everywhere, everyone thinks they know what mentoring is, and there is an intuitive belief that mentoring works."[15] Essentially, as Johnson and Ridley state, "mentoring is an act of generativity—a process of bringing into existence and passing on a professional legacy."[16]

In his book *The Third Third of Life*, Walter C. Wright promotes mentoring as a way to stay meaningfully engaged even in the later years of life. He says,

> Generativity is about investing ourselves in the next generation… Mentoring is an explicit example of generativity, with one person, usually older, making his or her life accessible as a resource to another seeking to realize his or her potential.[17]

From the standpoint of the mentor, the implication is that his or her acquired knowledge and skills need to be transmitted to others who can use them to help carry the workload in the present and continue the work in the future. From the perspective of the mentee, it is an opportunity to gain

---

15 Tammy D. Allen and Lillian Turner de Tormes Eby, *The Blackwell Handbook of Mentoring: A Multiple Perspectives Approach* (Malden, MA: Wiley-Blackwell, 2010), 7.

16 Johnson and Ridley, xi.

17 Walter C. Wright, Jr., *The Third Third of Life: Preparing for Your Future*, Kindle edition (Downers Grove, IL: IVP Books, 2012), locations 172–3.

access to the experience and knowledge resources of the mentor and build on those things so they can participate in taking their vocation or ministry to the next level. This desire to pass resources forward to following generations is common to all cultures. But the methods and means by which this is done are diverse. We will discuss a few of these and relate them to a model of ministry mentoring.

DEVELOPMENTAL AND SPONSORSHIP MENTORING

In the business world, there appear to be two approaches to mentoring: developmental mentoring and sponsorship mentoring. The developmental model focuses more on the development of the mentee while the sponsorship model focuses more on helping the mentee advance in his or her career. Mentoring relationships may include both aspects, but the primary focus is at issue. In practice, the mentee tends to drive the agenda of the developmental model, and the issue is how the mentee can benefit from the experience of the mentor, whereas in the sponsorship model the agenda tends to be driven by what the mentor can do for the mentee by his or her position. Both models may also be part of Christian ministry mentoring relationships, but the focus of this book is the developmental model.

As mentioned, developmental mentoring seeks primarily to assist a mentee in learning and skills development and allows any career advancement to occur naturally. An increase in knowledge and competence is the focus of developmental mentoring as opposed to the priorities that sponsorship mentoring may have.

To illustrate, we consider the biblical example of James and John, who requested to be placed at the right and left hand of Jesus in his kingdom (Mark 10:37). They were in effect seeking what sponsorship mentoring might provide—namely, power and position. But Jesus offered development mentoring, promoting character growth and ministry skills. So, in referring to the elements presented above, while not excluding them as possible options, mentoring activities such as providing sponsorship and giving mentees exposure and promoting their visibility may not necessarily be a primary concern of ministry mentoring.

FORMAL AND INFORMAL MENTORING

Formal mentoring relationships tend to be more structured and controlled, whereas informal mentoring relationships are more organic and spontaneous. Formal mentoring relationships are more intentional and intensive, while informal mentoring relationships are occasional and relaxed. Generally, mentoring relationships fall somewhere on the spectrum between the two, depending on the style of the mentor.

Informal	Blended Style (Enhanced Informal)	Formal
Organic	←――――→	Structured
Spontaneous	←――――→	Controlled
Occasional	←――――→	Intentional
Relaxed	←――――→	Intensive

Table 1: Mentoring Formality Spectrum

Where life and ministry modelling by the mentor is a part of the mentoring activities, the mentor may seek to spend time with the mentee in less controlled environments. These provide opportunities for the mentee to observe the mentor function in life and ministry. While these times are less structured and seem informal, they are no less intentional than other activities and form an important part of the complete mentoring experience.

In this book, our focus is on describing intentional mentorship relationships, which include the negotiating of mentoring agreements and therefore the description will tend toward the formal side of the spectrum. There may be some mentors and mentees who are not able to negotiate a mentoring agreement for various reasons yet still consider that they have a mentoring relationship. These arrangements have sometimes been called enhanced informal mentoring.[18]

PEER MENTORING

Peer mentoring is a relationship where the level of expertise is somewhat equivalent between those in the relationship. There is a large degree of common knowledge and experience but also opportunity to learn from peers with different skillsets. Those who are in peer mentoring relationships can adapt many of the mentoring principles and practices described in this book. Peers are "the most available source of relational empowerment, but the least developed."[19]

REVERSE MENTORING

Reverse mentoring occurs when the person who is generally less experienced has an area of expertise from which a more experienced person can learn. Earl Creps, in his book on the subject, suggests that it "assumes a completely opposite perspective on learning. While acknowledging the proven value of the older-to-younger approach (teaching down), it provides the vital complement of a younger-to-older method (teaching up)."[20] Many parents experience reverse mentoring when they need to ask their children how to use a computer or smartphone. The kids have somehow absorbed the intricacies of information technology and are able to guide their parents in the use of these new devices.

In a ministry context, younger people may have more experience in relating to their peers and can mentor an older person in the art of

---

18 Linda Philip-Jones, *The Mentor's Guide: How to Be the Kind of Mentor You Once Had—or Wish You'd Had*, (Grass Valley, CA: Coalition of Counselling Centers (CCC)/The Mentoring Group, 2003), 64.

19 Stanley and Clinton, 169. They describe types of peer relationships which include "acquaintance," "friend," and "close buddy" (173–87).

20 Earl G. Creps, *Reverse Mentoring: How Young Leaders Can Transform the Church and Why We Should Let Them* (San Francisco, CA: Jossey-Bass, 2008), xvii.

connecting with younger people. In organizational settings, such arrangements have helped to bridge generational gaps.

In mentoring relationships, mentors are also learners and can benefit greatly as they interact with their mentees and are exposed to different perspectives.[21]

The good mentor will, in any case, enter into a mentoring partnership with an openness to learn from his or her mentee. The honesty and humility demonstrated by the mentor's willingness to learn from the mentee can be a catalyst for a stronger relationship.

GROUP MENTORING

Group mentoring can take one of two forms. One scenario is that the mentee relates to several mentors at a time. This is sometimes referred to as "the personal board of directors" model of mentoring, or a mentoring constellation.[22] This could be used by someone coming into a leadership position that requires input from several mentors with different sets of expertise.

The other scenario is one mentor meeting with two or more mentees. This is more common. For mentors who are sought out by many mentees, this may be a strategic option to influence more mentees. Group sessions could be complemented by one-on-one sessions for maximum mentoring impact. As we read the gospels, we observe that this is the mentoring model Jesus used with his disciples. The early church fathers followed that

---

21   Lois J. Zachary, *The Mentor's Guide: Facilitating Effective Learning Relationships*, Kindle, second edition (San Francisco, CA: Jossey-Bass, 2012), location 2743.

22   Note that "mentoring constellation" here is used to denote a developmental network of experts (Ridley and Johnson, 93). This is not to be confused with what Stanley and Clinton call "the constellation model of mentoring" (157–68). Their use of the word speaks of a combination of upward mentoring, downward mentoring, and peer mentoring, which is a helpful way to understand relationships in ministry. It is not in the scope of this book to discuss it.

example.[23] In fact, it appears that most non-Western cultures demonstrate a preference to group approaches to mentoring. When a mentor uses this in a way that also pays attention to the individual needs in a group, it can add value to the mentees in ways that one-on-one mentoring cannot.

For instance, spiritual formation and effective leadership development necessarily assumes the need for people to develop the ability to live and work together in groups. It is in such contexts that leadership skills are developed to build ministry teams and community. Ministry skills are primarily about working with people, so taking a cue from the early church in this regard makes good sense. It must, however, be pointed out that the personal relationship of the mentor with an individual mentee or disciple should not be underplayed, as illustrated in the survey of Jesus' mentoring moments with Peter in Chapter Four. Thus, the effective mentor pays attention to both the individual mentees and the group dynamics of their interaction with each other. Additionally, group mentoring can provide a context where both men and women have access to mentoring in situations where one-on-one mentoring between a male and female may not be considered appropriate. I address this in more depth in Chapter Twelve.

EFFECTIVE AND INEFFECTIVE MENTORING

All of us mentor at one time or another. There are those who look to us for help in their lives, careers, or ministries. The question is whether we will mentor well or poorly.

The best way to consider this question relates to the learning objectives of the mentee. To the degree that we have helped the mentee achieve their learning objectives, we have been good mentors. To the extent that we have failed to guide them on their development journey, we have mentored ineffectively.

---

23   For instance, under Basil, "the monasteries and probably the hospice served as an indirect training center for those who would eventually be ordained. Finally, Basil, like Cyprian, valued gathering bishops together at least once a year to strengthen the unity of the church, to set apart leaders, and to deal with heresy. The council gave Basil an opportunity to influence and encourage the bishops, rendering it a form of mentoring in a group context" (Smither, 65).

However, it remains that the ownership of the learning rests primarily on the mentee. Some mentees may have ongoing issues in their lives that negatively impact the mentoring relationship.

A mentor can be said to have mentored poorly if he or she has failed to honour a mentoring agreement. Sometimes it is not a matter of poor mentoring. It may be a case of applying styles of mentoring which do not match certain situations. It can also be a case of incompatibility of mentor and mentee personalities.

However, we cannot overlook the possibility of toxic mentors, who for their own reasons may have a negative influence on their mentees. This can have the effect of reducing the mentees' suitability for ministry. A mentee who recognizes this should seek the best and quickest way to conclude the mentoring relationship. Chapter Eleven provides a guide for mentees who are looking for the right kind of mentors.

Let us review what those who mentor might look like:

- Excellent mentors are competent in their work.
- They continually grow in character and knowledge.
- They show consistent interest in the development of their mentees.
- They give of their time and make themselves available to their mentees.
- They also work at improving their mentoring skills.

FORMAL MINISTRY TRAINING AND MINISTRY MENTORING

Many ministers and pastors have had some formal training in biblical studies, theology, and practical ministry. As a part of that formal training, they may have participated in a ministry internship of some kind to gain hands-on experience. As helpful as such a practicum can be, it does not always fulfill the actual training needs for ministry. For that, an ongoing mentoring relationship can provide a fuller training experience after graduation. This relationship can continue even as the person has begun their particular ministry assignment. We will see the benefits of such a relationship throughout this book.

A person supervising an intern may also want to structure the relationship to be a mentoring relationship, as we have described. Online and distance education are increasingly becoming the training delivery mode of choice. A mentoring program built around such education initiatives promises to strengthen the learning experience for students. The challenge may be to find mentors who have the necessary mentoring skills and available time to spend with such students.[24]

There are also those in ministry who may not have the benefit of formal training for various reasons. In such cases, a mentoring relationship is even more crucial and would include providing the training and resources that a formal training might have provided.

The shortage of formal training opportunities is not unusual when we consider some periods in the history of the church. For instance, early Protestant ministry training in North America was primarily built around mentorship. Craig van Gelder, in his book *The Missional Church and Leadership Formation*, explains that the normal practice of training pastors for congregational leadership at the beginning of nineteenth-century America "was to associate with a mentor who could provide exposure to ministry and guidance in how to read the Bible and how to prepare sermons."[25]

In *Theological Education Matters*, Linda Cannell describes the nature of early pastoral training methods, writing that "pastor-tutors" were sought out by students to be trained by them for church ministry.[26] This association of students with active pastors in "parsonage seminary" settings afforded the students opportunity to be trained in ministry contexts even though the theological education piece was inadequate. Cannell explains further:

---

[24] This book can be used to train potential mentors, but they will still need to make the time.

[25] Craig Van Gelder, *The Missional Church and Leadership Formation: Helping Congregations Develop Leadership Capacity*, Missional Church Series (Grand Rapids, MI: W.B. Eerdmans Pub. Co., 2009), 20.

[26] Linda Cannell, *Theological Education Matters: Leadership Education for the Church* (Newburgh, IN: EDCOT Press, 2006), 140–1.

The dominant model for professional education through the seventeenth and eighteenth centuries was apprenticeship. This mode ultimately proved unworkable, as the complexity and knowledge base of the professions increased and as the number of willing masters decreased. The professional had enough to do without taking on an apprentice. Also, the strength of the apprentice relationship was also its weakness: ministers in training were influenced by the idiosyncrasies of their mentor. In time, training was taken over by full-time teachers in professional schools, which had the effect of removing the student from the field. Since professional schools tend to be expensive, the shift from apprenticeship to formal schooling with an internship also limited access to professional fields.[27]

An apprenticeship model of ministry training and a formal education are both deficient when they stand alone. When the student can experience both, the learning outcomes are significantly better.

This is corroborated in the development and education of other professions as well. For instance, Klasen and Clutterbuck in their book on mentoring in organizational contexts state that "formal education and induction training alone do not fully prepare individuals for the world of work; continuous learning by way of a variety of learning methods is the only way to achieve maximum performance."[28]

Mentoring, as a training method, is customizable and enables learners to apply knowledge and skills in their immediate context under the guidance of mentors who have life and work experience. As Clinton and Clinton write in *The Mentoring Handbook*, "One of the special pluses of mentoring is that though it is an informal mode of training, it can be adapted to supplement formal and non-formal modes."[29]

---

27 Ibid., 190–1.
28 Nadine Klasen and David Clutterbuck, *Implementing Mentoring Schemes: A Practical Guide to Successful Programs* (Oxford, UK: Butterworth-Heinemann, 2002), 3.
29 J. Robert Clinton and Dr. Richard Clinton, *The Mentoring Handbook: Detailed Guidelines and Helps for Christian Mentors and Mentorees* (Altadena, CA: Barnabas Publishers, 1991), 1–1.

To conclude this part of the discussion, let me suggest that whenever possible, prospective ministers should seek and avail themselves of any opportunities for formal education in biblical studies, theology, and practical ministry. But as they do this, they should also find mentors to help them apply their "school learning" in specific ministry contexts. If there are no schooling opportunities, at least they should search for ministry mentors to guide them in their ministry journeys. Those mentors may need to focus a little more on playing the role of a teacher or instructor in biblical studies and theology while at the same being ministry mentors in all the other areas discussed in this book. However, whenever possible the mentor should direct the mentee toward formal ministry training opportunities as they become available.

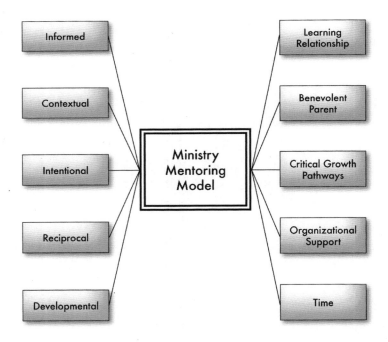

Figure 2: Components of the Ministry Mentoring Model

A CHRISTIAN MINISTRY MENTORING MODEL

Now that we have a basic understanding of what we mean by ministry mentoring, I want to outline some of the themes around the ministry mentoring model that form the framework of this book. Some of these I have described briefly earlier in this chapter, but it will be helpful to see them in the broader context. Figure 2 presents these themes in graphic form to assist us in understanding how they fit together. An expanded version of this graphic can be seen in Appendix C.

1. Since mentoring is a universal concept, we acknowledge that our understanding of mentoring is *informed* by Scripture, by history, by leadership studies relating to various vocations, and by practical experiences.
2. Ministry mentoring is adaptable into different *contexts*, national and ethnic cultures, as well as different kinds of church communities.
3. The ministry mentoring model we are promoting assumes *intentionality* in initiating and sustaining mentoring relationships, whether formally structured or informally arranged. This intentionality applies both to controlled environments and less controlled environments.
4. According to this model, mentoring relationships are *reciprocal* connections between mentors and mentees. These are one-on-one relationships which group mentoring can augment when warranted. These are usually face-to-face but can also include two-way exchanges through letters, email, and other means of communication provided there is an element of give and take.
5. The priority of this model is the growth and *development* of the mentee in both character and competency. The character aspect relates to spiritual growth and the competency aspect relates to the development of ministry skills.

6. In this model, mentoring is a *learning relationship* that the mentee drives. He or she sets the learning agenda through their learning needs and areas of interest. The mentor's primary role is to guide, to provide resources, and to facilitate the learning process.
7. This ministry mentoring model uses the analogy of a *benevolent parent* who has a generous attitude toward his or her child and does whatever it takes to assist the child in their development. The model includes the ability to balance nurturance and discipline in an appropriate manner. In the same way, the mentoring relationship is primarily for the benefit of the mentee. As the child matures, the relationship with the parent progresses until the two relate to each other as adults. Similarly, the mentor-mentee relationship potentially progresses toward a peer mentoring relationship. An important piece of this theme is the *mutual trust* between the mentor and mentee.
8. *Critical growth pathways* are learning activities and strategies that arise out of the mentoring agenda. They are essential to helping the ministry mentee get to the next level and advance the development of the mentee leader. These are also influenced by *divine activity* in the life of the mentee and provide the basis for the development plan which the mentor customizes to the needs of the mentees.
9. *Organizational support* is a part of a healthy ministry mentoring model. Where possible, an initiative by the leadership team of an organization facilitates mentoring relationships through the appointment of a mentoring coordinator and a mentor training program. Mentees are encouraged to create developmental networks or a constellation of mentors to meet their learning needs.
10. Mentoring that is in any way intentional needs to address the issue of *time*. At the inception of a mentoring relationship, the mentor and mentee need to negotiate the length of the relationship. Both will need to consider how much

time they need to invest in the mentoring relationship on an ongoing basis. They will need to adjust other areas of their schedules accordingly.

In the next three chapters, we will look at mentoring through the lens of Scripture and see how various examples of mentoring activities in the Bible point us toward a biblical model of ministry mentoring.

QUESTIONS: FROM REFLECTION TO ACTION

1. What are the different ways you have experienced mentoring?
2. From your experiences, what are some things you would like to implement when you mentor others?
3. From your experiences, what are some things you would like to avoid having your mentees experience?
4. What do you think is the best way to combine theological and ministry training with mentoring?
5. What aspect of the ministry model stands out to you?
6. How has your understanding of ministry mentoring changed through reading this chapter? What will you now do differently?

Chapter Three

MENTORING IN THE OLD TESTAMENT

Elijah wanted to die. He felt that he had done everything he could. He had prayed fire down from heaven in the sight of the people and still did not feel his ministry was successful.

> "I have had enough, Lord," he said. "Take my life; I am no better than my ancestors."
>
> —1 Kings 19:4

God let him rest awhile but told him that he wasn't finished yet. One of the things he needed to do was to anoint a successor. So he found Elisha and invited him to follow him.

We don't know how long Elisha followed Elijah, nor do we have many details about that mentoring relationship. But we do know that at the end, Elisha understood the significance of anointing Elijah. He wanted a double portion of the Spirit that was on Elijah and intentionally pursued that until the end. The biblical narrative records that twice as many miracles happened through Elisha, an indication that he received what he had pursued.

There are at least two mentoring lessons to be learned from that story. First, Elisha took the initiative to get from his mentor what he felt he needed. Second, Elijah had the capacity to mentor someone who ultimately exceeded him. Thus, we see the attitude of the mentee who eagerly wanted to receive everything he could and the attitude of the mentor who was willing to let the mentee become greater than the mentor.

We can find many other biblical examples of mentoring-type activities, attitudes, and relationships. This is to be expected, since mentoring is a universal part of human interaction. We do not have to consider it unusual to see examples of mentoring in the biblical stories where we have not seen them before, because mentoring is simply a part of human relationships, no matter how we label it. Surprising little hints in those stories often point to important principles of mentoring. From those signs, we can discover a biblical and theological basis for the practice of ministry mentoring. As those who are interested in ministry mentoring, we are naturally curious about how someone like Moses mentored Joshua and how Paul mentored Timothy.

In this chapter, we will survey some of the leading mentoring examples in the Old Testament. In the following two chapters, we will look at mentoring stories and principles in the New Testament. Let us begin with God, who is the master designer of everything good, including mentoring relationships.

IN THE BEGINNING, GOD...

God is a relational being and has created us to be relational beings. God relates to us, and we relate to each other, in community. The creation narratives allude to this concept and form the basis of the biblical story from beginning to end.

God, the Original Mentor

The nature of the relationship God has with humankind is one of purposeful partnership. How does God relate to his human partners? He has created them for a purpose. They are happiest as they move toward fulfilling that purpose, and God is pleased. Under God's administration of his world, humankind is to have a stewarding dominion over the created order. But to fulfill that purpose, they need to stay in a relationship with God because he is the source of knowledge and all the resources they need for life and work.

The first mentoring relationship in the Bible is between God and Adam. We see this when we consider the task of naming the animals which

God gave to him (Genesis 2:19). This is what a good mentor would do to encourage development: release the mentee to undertake a project and then take an interest in the outcome.[30]

The patriarchal narratives describe this pattern of divine interaction with the fathers of the ancient Jewish nation. For instance, God invited Abraham to deliberate with him concerning the judgment on Sodom (Genesis 18:16–33).[31] This pattern is also repeatedly demonstrated throughout the rest of Scripture and history as God continually called human beings into a partnership with him to fulfill his purposes.[32] As I have reflected on this, I have come to the conclusion that a ministry mentor's understanding of how God relates to them will be mirrored in how they relate to their mentees.

Mission of God as the Purpose of Ministry

We understand that an ultimate goal lies behind ministry mentoring relationships. As Christians, we affirm that ministry necessarily exists in service of God's kingdom purposes in that the mission of God is to reconcile the world to God. Scripture states that God the Father *"reconciled us to himself through Christ and gave us the ministry of reconciliation"* (2 Corinthians 5:18). The ministry of Christians, then, is to make the world aware of what God has done through the crucifixion and resurrection of Christ. We embody the good news that the kingdom of God has come and is coming. Ministry mentoring is formed by that underlying truth, and with that as its focus it facilitates the development of the knowledge, skills, and attitudes of mentees so that they can each fulfill their unique roles in the kingdom purposes of God.

---

30 The second example of a mentoring encounter in the Bible occurs between the serpent and Eve (Genesis 3:1–5). In this case, the serpent sought to do harm to Adam and Eve through a mentoring conversation which ultimately led to the fall of humanity. This illustrates that mentoring can be used to destroy.

31 Other examples in the patriarchal narratives include Genesis 22:1–12; 28:10–22; and 32:22–30.

32 For instance, see Exodus 3–4; 14:10–17; 17:1–7; 32:9–14; Deuteronomy 6; Joshua 1:1–9; Judges 2:1–4; 2 Kings 13:14–19; Isaiah 1:18–20; et al.

Team Building and Succession Planning

A primary impetus for mentoring is the awareness of one's human limitations and mortality. A person who mentors another recognizes that she does not have the capability to fulfill current responsibilities and will not live long enough to accomplish everything she believes needs to be done. So she will want to equip those around her to access their energy and capabilities to help address current realities. At the same time, she will want to transfer her faith and ministry skills to the next generation so that the next generation can build on what they have received and take it to another level. As such, mentoring is a critical component of both *team building* and *succession planning*. Mentoring, accordingly, is a generative activity by which the mentor multiplies herself for wider and longer impact.

Accepting our limitations establishes the wisdom of reproducing ourselves by training and mentoring those who will work alongside us. Jethro advised Moses along those lines when he suggested that Moses teach the people and show them how to live, but he also suggested that Moses select capable men and have them serve as judges for the simple cases so Moses would only need to deal with the difficult situations. Jethro then stated, *"That will make your load lighter, because they will share it with you"* (Exodus 18:22).

Acknowledging our mortality leads to the practice of equipping and empowering those who will outlive us to carry on the work we have begun. The psalmist expresses the same sentiment: *"Teach us to number our days, that we may gain a heart of wisdom"* (Psalm 90:12). The pattern in the biblical record that demonstrates this notion of transferring faith, knowledge, expertise, and authority is a strong rationale for the practice of ministry mentoring. I address this dual theme further in the conclusion.

Reading the Examples of Ministry Mentoring in Scripture

Biblical examples of intentional mentoring activities are primarily descriptive and not necessarily prescriptive. However, they are instructive and can inform our theology of ministry mentoring.

For everything that was written in the past was written to teach us, so that through the endurance taught in the Scriptures and the encouragement they provide we might have hope.

—Romans 15:4[33]

In other words, we study the stories in Scripture and observe what was going on in the different mentoring relationships. We may then take and apply to our context whatever principles are appropriate. Of course, we may not see all the detailed information we might like to see, but we can read those stories with God's greater story in view and see how the smaller stories mirror his relationship with humanity. I believe each of these examples suggests one or more aspects of mentoring which we can integrate into our overall understanding of ministry mentoring.

MOSES AND MENTORING

While the practice of mentoring was a part of human experience from the beginning, we can see a more obvious scriptural illustration of mentoring in the leadership experiences of Moses. His early education was in Egypt in the household of Pharaoh (Acts 7:22). He undertook later life training under the tutelage of his father-in-law, Jethro, who was the priest of Midian. Jethro had a relationship with Moses in which he felt free to give the kind of advice a mentor might provide. As we have already seen, he helped Moses understand how to delegate his responsibilities and multiply his leadership capabilities by empowering others to take some of the burdens of leadership (Exodus 18:18–24).

Moses and Joshua

As Moses began his assignment of leading the nation of Israel through the wilderness toward the Promised Land, he chose Joshua as his assistant. From the few interactions about which we can read, we observe some significant mentoring activities that contributed to Joshua's development as a leader. The transfer of leadership from Moses to Joshua, and the role

---

33 See also 2 Timothy 3:16.

mentorship played in that transfer, is a primary Old Testament example of how a younger leader grew under the watchful eye of an experienced leader. In *The Joshua Portrait*, Katherine Haubert and Robert Clinton suggest that "Joshua provides a good biblical model for leadership development under mentoring influence."[34] The transition from Moses to Joshua, they add, was one of the "few biblical models of successful leadership transition... Joshua, the leader, emerged as a product of sovereign intentions, life experiences, and quality mentoring through Moses."[35]

Joshua first appears in the narrative when he was assigned to marshal an army and fight the Amalekites (Exodus 17:8–16). He may have already been a part of Moses' leadership team, but this was surely an event that had potential to bring him closer to Moses. The battle was also being fought on a spiritual plane, as seen by Moses raising the staff of God over his head as a symbol of God's presence with the people in the battle. When it was over, the record showed that *"Joshua overcame the Amalekite army with the sword"* (Exodus 17:13). God's presence, Moses' holding up the staff of God with the help of Aaron and Hur, and Joshua's capable military leadership won the day. Here it appears that God was already sovereignly positioning Joshua as Moses' successor.

Joshua's journey up the mountain with Moses gave him an opportunity to observe Moses in the presence of God (Exodus 24:9–18).[36] Though it may not have been intentional, Moses was modelling for Joshua the importance of intimacy with God. When Joshua came into leadership, he followed in that same kind of relationship with God (Joshua 5:13–15).

We can see other mentoring events in the narrative. For instance, on one occasion Joshua received a lesson in discernment:

Moses turned and went down the mountain with the two tablets of the covenant law in his hands...

---

[34] Katherine Haubert and J. Robert Clinton, *The Joshua Portrait: A Study in Leadership Development, Leadership Transition, and Destiny Fulfillment* (Altadena, CA: Barnabas Publishers, 1990), 3.

[35] Ibid., 5, 9.

[36] See also Exodus 33:11.

> *When Joshua heard the noise of the people shouting, he said to Moses, "There is the sound of war in the camp."*
> *Moses replied: "It is not the sound of victory, it is not the sound of defeat; it is the sound of singing that I hear."*
> —Exodus 32:15, 17–18

Moses had previously heard from God that Israel had turned to idol worship and had already discerned that the noise in the camp was revelry related to idolatry (Exodus 32:7–8).

On another occasion, Joshua received a situational lesson concerning the operation of the Spirit in the case of the men prophesying in the camp. He wanted to rebuke them because they appeared to be insubordinate, but Moses demonstrated a different attitude: *"Are you jealous for my sake? I wish that all the Lord's people were prophets and that the Lord would put his Spirit on them!"* (Numbers 11:29) Here Moses also modelled humility and a willingness to see others empowered.

As his final mentoring act, Moses passed the leadership to Joshua and gave final instructions and encouragement.[37] After his death, Moses' writings (the book of the law) were not only God-inspired instructions for the people but they became a continual reminder of Moses' mentoring for Joshua. God referred Joshua to these writings, saying, *"Keep this Book of the Law always on your lips; meditate on it day and night, so that you may be careful to do everything written in it. Then you will be prosperous and successful"* (Joshua 1:8).

Moses and the Next Generation

Moses, in his last address as leader of the people, highlighted the urgency of transferring faith to the next generation, specifically suggesting various mentoring activities that would impact those who receive the training:

> *Love the Lord your God with all your heart and with all your soul and with all your strength. These commandments that I give you today are to be on your hearts. Impress them on your children. Talk about them when you sit at home and when you walk along the road, when you lie down and*

---

37 Numbers 27:18–23; Deuteronomy 1:38; 3:21, 28; and 31:1–30.

when you get up. Tie them as symbols on your hands and bind them on your foreheads. Write them on the doorframes of your houses and on your gates.

—Deuteronomy 6:5–9[38]

These instructions demonstrate the importance of intentional mentoring for posterity. Efficiently transferring faith to the next generation is the ultimate objective of ministry mentoring. It takes godly leaders who are called to serve God in ministry to consistently hold the ideals of faith before the people so that they will not fade away. Similarly, the psalmist says,

He decreed statutes for Jacob and established the law in Israel, which he commanded our ancestors to teach their children, so the next generation would know them, even the children yet to be born, and they in turn would tell their children.

—Psalm 78:5–6

MENTORING RELATIONSHIPS IN THE OLD TESTAMENT

There are occasional hints of mentoring relationships in the Old Testament, though they are not described in depth. There is mention of groups of prophets who are associated with Samuel and Elisha.[39] The Israelite institutions of the writing prophets, the scribal tradition, and the sages in the wisdom tradition were involved in the communication of divine revelation in various forms.[40] This process involved the intimacy of master and disciple relationships.[41] Some of these relationships are illustrated in the following Old Testament mentoring stories.

---

38 See also Deuteronomy 4:9, where he says, *"Teach them to your children and to their children after them."*

39 1 Samuel 19:20–24; 2 Kings 4:1, 38; and 9:1.

40 Isaiah 8:16; 54:13; Jeremiah 36:32; Ezra 7:6, 11; Proverbs 22:17; 25:1; and Jeremiah 18:18.

41 M.J. Wilkins, "Disciples and Discipleship," ed. Joel B. Green, Jeannine K. Brown, and Nicholas Perrin, *Dictionary of Jesus and the Gospels*, second edition (Downers Grove, IL; Nottingham, England: IVP Academic; IVP, 2013), 202.

Naomi and Ruth

We find a beautiful story which anticipates the ancestry of King David in the book of Ruth. It describes how Naomi helped her widowed Moabite daughter-in-law Ruth navigate her way in the environment of Israelite culture and religion. She was a mentor to Ruth in the process of finding another husband and home where she could rest and raise a family (Ruth 3:1–5). The very fact that Ruth opted to follow Naomi to a nation where she would be a foreigner is testament to the relationship of trust which is essential between a mentor and mentee. Naomi demonstrated concern for Ruth and guided her toward a future that was right for Ruth in the first instance, similarly satisfying for Naomi, and ultimately good for the kingdom.

Eli and Samuel

The failure of Eli to mentor his sons into faithful ministry provides a negative example, where an older generation failed to transfer faith and godly character to the next generation (1 Samuel 2:22–36). Eli, however, had mentoring success with Samuel in helping him to hear God's voice and encouraging him to speak the divinely revealed words that prophesied the destruction of Eli's household (1 Samuel 3:9). We also find here a biblical example of reverse mentoring where a younger, less experienced person had something to contribute to an older wiser person who was ready to receive it. This relationship did not have at its priority the concerns of the mentor or the needs of the mentee. The focus was on God and his purposes.[42]

David and Solomon

King David also may not have had great success in mentoring his older sons or with maintaining order in his household among his children (2 Samuel 13, 15), but he seems to have had some success with a younger son, Solomon, who would become his successor. King David had it in his heart to build a temple to the Lord, but the Lord told him that he was not the one to

---

42 There are several other mentoring relationships which could be mentioned in this time period. Samuel was a mentor to Saul and then to David. Jonathan and David were in a peer mentoring relationship. David had counsellors (wise men) and prophets who functioned like a constellation of mentors.

build it. Rather, his son Solomon would build that temple. So David spent time with Solomon instructing him how to build the temple, imparting skills, and empowering him with all he needed for the task (1 Chronicles 28:9–28). But something which may not be evident on a surface reading of the scriptures is the mentoring that Solomon received relating to other areas of life.

In the book of the Proverbs, Solomon often refers to life instructions he received from his father. An example of such a reference states,

> *For I too was a son to my father, still tender, and cherished by my mother. Then he taught me, and he said to me, "Take hold of my words with all your heart; keep my commands, and you will live."*
> —Proverbs 4:3–4[43]

It appears that Solomon would have received much wisdom as a result of the mentoring influence of his father and mother. The book of Chronicles also records that *"Jonathan, David's uncle, was a counselor, being a man of understanding and a scribe. He and Jehiel the son of Hachmoni attended the king's sons"* (1 Chronicles 27:32, ESV). Solomon, as one of those sons, propagated the collection of proverbs which became a mentoring manual for Israel and us (1 Kings 4:32 and Ecclesiastes 12:9).

Elijah and Elisha

We get a brief glimpse of another mentoring relationship in Elijah and Elisha (1 Kings 19:19–21 and 2 Kings 2). Elijah, after his bout with depression when he expressed his wish to die, was instructed by God to anoint Elisha as his successor to carry on his ministry. The Moses and Joshua relationship was similar in that the same Hebrew word for "assistant" is used to describe that relationship.[44] The biblical authors use this word to denote

---

43 Other such references include Proverbs 1:8; 2:1; 3:1–2; 3:11; 3:21; 4:1; 4:10; and 5:1.

44 *šārēt* (Hebrew).

those who served an important person or leader.[45] This is not the word for ordinary service.[46] Both Joshua and Elisha succeeded their former masters. The proximity lent itself to being mentored by their leaders and ultimately they became their leaders' successors.

Mentor-mentee relationships in the Ancient Near East included the element of mentees serving the mentor. This association ultimately contributed to the credibility of the mentee/assistant. For instance, King Jehoshaphat of Judah was looking for a credible prophet through whom he and his coalition partners (the king of Israel and the king of Edom) might inquire of the Lord concerning a dire situation in battle. One of the Israelite king's servants suggested to him Elisha, the son of Shaphat. As a credential, they added that Elisha had *"poured water on the hands of Elijah"* (2 Kings 3:11, ESV), indicating that while the well-known Elijah was no longer around, his successor and former mentee was available to serve God and the faithful King Jehoshaphat in the same spirit.

The biblical narrative does not provide any information about how Elijah mentored Elisha. We read about how Elijah called him by putting his cloak on him, and then how Elisha left his parents' household and followed him. Much later in the story, when it was time for Elijah to ascend to heaven (the Spirit had revealed this to the whole prophetic school), Elisha was adamant on following Elijah until the very end. His persistence was that of a model mentee who knew how to extract the best and the most out of a mentoring relationship. Elijah asked him what he wanted and Elisha replied by asking for a double portion of his spirit upon him. Elijah continued to test his resolve by telling Elisha that he would get what he desired if he witnessed Elijah as he departed from him. Elisha persisted and received (2 Kings 2:1–15).

---

45 R. Laird Harris, Gleason L. Archer, and Bruce K. Waltke, eds., *Theological Wordbook of the Old Testament*, electronic edition (Chicago, IL: Moody Press, 1999), reference 2472.

46 The word for that is *ebed*.

Mordechai and Esther

Another example of a mentoring relationship is that of Mordechai mentoring his cousin Esther. He had a profound influence on Esther's life and career, and ultimately as saviour of her nation. He advised her on how to best survive an environment which was hostile to the Jewish people—namely, to keep her nationality hidden. Later, once she had gained favour, he counselled her on the urgency of saving her nation from imminent destruction even if it meant revealing her identity.[47]

In this chapter, we have looked at several Old Testament examples of mentoring activities. These do not provide a full sense of what mentoring relationships looked like in those times, yet they give us a taste of some of the ways in which ministry skills were transferred forward to the next generation.

To get a more complete picture, we have many New Testament examples of mentoring activities and relationships, particularly in the ministry of Jesus with his disciples and in the various relationships Paul had with his apostolic teams and churches. We will look at these in the next two chapters.

QUESTIONS: FROM REFLECTION TO ACTION

1. What happened to the generation after Joshua, who was mentored by Moses? What steps do we need to take to avoid a Book of Judges scenario?
2. What happened to the generation after Solomon, who was mentored by David? What lessons can we learn from the decline of the house of David?
3. What was the secret behind the generational success story of the Rekabites in Jeremiah 35:1–10? What can we do to emulate that success?
4. What have you learned from the Old Testament examples of mentoring that you want to implement in your mentorship? What steps will you take?

---

47   Esther 2:5, 10–11,19–20; 4:12–14.

Chapter Four

HOW DID JESUS MENTOR?

Before Jesus arrived on the scene, we have the fascinating stories of Elizabeth and Mary. First, Elizabeth, who all her life was unable to conceive, became pregnant even though she was advanced in years. This took place after the angel Gabriel announced to her husband, Zechariah the priest, that this was going to happen (Luke 1:5–25).

Six months later, Gabriel appeared to Mary, who was not yet married but engaged to a man named Joseph, and announced that she was going to conceive a child miraculously who was to be named Jesus. The angel mentioned to Mary that Elizabeth her cousin was also going to have a baby in her old age, which in itself was a miracle (Luke 1:26–38). In this way, the angel provided an opportunity for Mary to be connected to another human being for mentoring support.

Mary went to visit Elizabeth and received a divinely inspired affirmation concerning what she had experienced. Elizabeth functioned as a mentor to her younger cousin at a crucial point in Mary's life (Luke 1:39–45). This mentoring connection is significant. It helps us to understand the need for godly mentorship during times when the mentee experiences unusual divine encounters and revelations. A mentor can help the mentee work through such experiences when others may not understand what is happening. Consider what Mary would have missed if Elizabeth had not been in her life at that time.

JESUS AS MENTOR OF THE APOSTLES

During the time of Jesus, it was not unusual for a leading rabbi to have a following of disciples. These master-disciple relationships were the means by which emerging rabbis received their education in Judaism. Jesus adopted this format to express the kind of relationship he would develop with his followers, "but he would mould and shape it to form a unique form of discipleship, far different than others."[48]

Jesus' model of disciple-making, for the purposes of this book, is essentially ministry mentoring as observed in the gospels.

> *He appointed twelve that they might be with him and that he might send them out to preach and to have authority to drive out demons.*
> —Mark 3:14–15

Jesus was very intentional and deliberate in his training of the twelve apostles.[49] A.B. Bruce, in his book *The Training of the Twelve*, observes that the gospels present Jesus beginning "at a very early period of His ministry to gather round Him a company of disciples, with a view to the preparation of an agency for carrying on the work of the divine kingdom."[50] The twelve he selected were to be

> something more than travelling companions or menial servants of the Lord Jesus Christ. They were to be, in the meantime, students of Christian doctrine, occasional fellow-labourers in the work of the kingdom, and eventually Christ's chosen trained agents for propagating the faith after he himself had left the earth.[51]

---

48   Wilkins, 203.
49   Two books have demonstrated this extensively: Alexander Balmain Bruce, *The Training of the Twelve; or, Passages out of the Gospels, Exhibiting the Twelve Disciples of Jesus under Discipline for the Apostleship* (Oak Harbor, WA: Logos Research Systems, Inc., 1995) and Robert Emerson Coleman and Roy J. Fish, *The Master Plan of Evangelism*, thirtieth anniversary edition (Grand Rapids, MI: F.H. Revell, 1993).
50   Bruce, 12.
51   Ibid., 30.

Robert Emerson Coleman's classic *Master Plan of Evangelism* can easily be read as a description of Jesus doing ministry mentoring. In answering the question of why Jesus focused on a few rather than the multitudes, Coleman points out that

> Jesus was not trying to impress the crowd, but to usher in a kingdom. This meant that he needed people who could lead the multitudes... Before the world could ever be permanently helped, people would have to be raised up who could lead the multitudes in the things of God.[52]

Let us consider ten principles Jesus demonstrated in ministry mentoring with his disciples.[53]

1. CAREFUL SELECTION

Jesus carefully selected and enlisted those he was going to train and send into the world to carry on his work. He selected them after prayerful consideration. The selection was based not on educational qualifications but on a willingness to spend time with Jesus as he called them to follow him (Matthew 4:19–20). Even later, after the resurrection of Christ when they launched into their ministry, the religious authorities observed *"that [Peter and John] were unschooled, ordinary men... and they took note that these men had been with Jesus"* (Acts 4:13). He limited those he selected to a manageable number of twelve (Luke 6:13–17). He also selected a smaller group of three—Peter, James, and John—who were invited to deeper interaction with Jesus than the other disciples.[54]

The implications for ministry mentoring are that a mentor, while serving in ministry for the benefit of many, should carefully select those on whom he will focus more attention for leadership development. The

---

52 Coleman and Fish, 28–9.
53 The first eight of the principles have been adapted from Robert Coleman. I have identified two additional principles.
54 Matthew 17:1; Mark 5:37; and 14:33.

mentor is well advised to be prayerfully selective so that he will ultimately have those as mentees who are divinely suited for the given time. However, the fact that Judas the betrayer was also among those who Jesus selected can help the mentor to discern that even if we take precautions in the selection process, the mentee may ultimately choose a different path.

2. INTENTIONAL ASSOCIATION

Jesus invited the disciples to follow him wherever he was going. He spent quality time with them so they could get to know him. They were selected so that they could *"be with him"* (Mark 3:14). The disciples had opportunities to observe him in a variety of contexts so they could see how he ministered and reacted in different life and ministry situations. They had opportunities to hear him teach and could ask questions to clarify what they did not understand.

> *He did not say anything to them without using a parable. But when he was alone with his own disciples, he explained everything.*
> —Mark 4:34[55]

As the time of his departure approached, Jesus spent more and more private time with the twelve to impress on them the message of the kingdom of God.[56]

The implications for ministry mentoring are that the mentor will do well to structure her time to provide enough opportunity to associate with the mentee in life and ministry contexts. It is in these different contexts that issues relating to the learning journey of the mentee will naturally emerge and the mentor can address them.

---

55   See also Matthew 13:10 and 18:1.
56   Matthew 20:17ff; John 11:54; and 13–17.

3. CALL TO COMMITMENT

Jesus called his disciples to obedience and sacrifice. The more they heard his teaching as his disciples and designated apostles, the better they understood what that meant. Ultimately they were to be ready to lay down their lives as Jesus did. Jesus expected total commitment. He made the cost of this commitment clear to them when he said, *"Whoever wants to be my disciple must deny themselves and take up their cross daily and follow me"* (Luke 9:23). There did not seem to be room for an on-again-off-again relationship. To those who thought they might want it both ways, he said, *"No one who puts a hand to the plow and looks back is fit for service in the kingdom of God"* (Luke 9:62). He spoke these words to the crowd, but they had clear implications for his inner circle of disciples, who had left everything to follow Jesus (Mark 10:2).

In a formal ministry mentoring relationship, the commitment level needs to be high in both the mentor and mentee. A mentor will want to invest time in those who are willing to pay the price.

4. SPIRITUAL IMPARTATION

Jesus poured his life into the lives of his disciples in many ways. He loved them completely and withheld nothing that would add value to their ministry. Jesus gave them the secrets of the kingdom. He vested them with authority. His mission became their mission, and to fulfill it he imparted to them his Holy Spirit. Just as some of the Spirit who was upon Moses was transferred to the seventy elders and then to Joshua, and as the Spirit who was on Elijah was transferred to Elisha, so Jesus imparted the Spirit to his disciples.[57] The Holy Spirit became for them the heavenly Mentor and the source of power to do even greater things than they had seen Jesus do (John 14:12).

As the mentee matures, the mentor will gradually impart knowledge, experience, and wisdom without holding back. While the mentor cannot give the Holy Spirit as Jesus does, the mentee can nonetheless receive a

---

57 Numbers 11:25; 27:18, 20; Deuteronomy 34:9; 2 Kings 2:9, 15; John 20:21; and Acts 1:8.

spiritual impartation through prayer and association (2 Timothy 1:6 and Romans 1:11).

5. EXEMPLARY DEMONSTRATION

Jesus was an example to the disciples, showing them how to live and nurture a relationship with the heavenly Father through prayer and obedience. In his public ministry, he demonstrated to them how to relate to people and evangelize. They had many opportunities to observe how Jesus healed the sick and cast out demons. They heard him preach and teach as he applied scriptures to life situations. They were going to continue his ministry after his departure, so they needed ample opportunity to observe him in action. As followers of the way of Jesus, they needed to know how to do things the way he did them. The four gospels are, in large part, a record of Jesus' demonstration of ministry activity and the pattern upon which his disciples continued the ministry he began (Acts 1:1).

Mentoring of this kind does not take place just in the office or classroom but the field of ministry. The mentor needs to demonstrate how ministry is done and then take the time to explain what happens. Including the mentees in this way requires the mentor to be vulnerable to them. While we are not perfect as the Lord Jesus, "our weaknesses need not impair discipleship when shining through them is a transparent sincerity to follow Christ."[58]

6. DELEGATION OF RESPONSIBILITIES

Jesus gave the disciples opportunity to minister, giving them ministry assignments as well as tasks related to the maintenance of the group. By the time he finished his earthly ministry, their practical experience, in conjunction with the impartation of the Holy Spirit, had provided what was needed to fulfill the mission.

For example, on one occasion Jesus sent the twelve out on a mission with full authority and detailed instructions, and when they returned Jesus

---

58   Coleman and Fish, 69.

gave them the opportunity to debrief (Luke 9:1–6, 10). He followed a similar pattern with an expanded group of seventy-two (Luke 10:1–12, 17–20). These mission advances were initially restricted to *"the lost sheep of the house of Israel"* (Matthew 10:6, ESV). But after his resurrection, he commissioned them for a global mission (Matthew 28:18–20).

The implication of delegation for a ministry mentoring context is that the mentee cannot just be taught, affirmed, and encouraged but must also be launched into ministry action with full empowerment.

7. SUPERVISION OF MINISTRY

The disciples reported to Jesus concerning their ministry activities (Mark 6:30 and Luke 9:10). There were frequent conversations and interactions with Jesus whereby he monitored, corrected, and enhanced their understanding of the kingdom and how they needed to live in it and advance it. The debriefings demonstrated accountability to Jesus and provided an opportunity for course corrections and attitude adjustments.[59]

A ministry mentoring relationship involves accountability conversations where the mentor engages the mentee on performance and quality control for ministry excellence.

8. EXPECTATION OF FRUITFULNESS

Jesus expected fruitfulness in ministry. He expected that his disciples' ministry should produce results. For example, on one occasion when they were unable to cast the demon out of a boy, Jesus expressed his frustration: *"O faithless and twisted generation, how long am I to be with you? How long am I to bear with you? Bring him here to me"* (Matthew 17:17, ESV). He rebuked the demon, healed the boy, and later explained to his disciples the reasons for their inability to minister effectively in this case (Matthew 17:20 and Mark 9:29). The parable of the talents illustrates the same kind of expectation: faithful engagement of the servant (or minister) leads to good outcomes while faithlessness leads to fruitlessness (Matthew 25:14–30).

---

59 Matthew 13:36–43; 16:5–28; 18:1–5; and 19:23–29.

So it follows that Jesus was keenly interested in an outcome where his disciples would multiply themselves as followers of Christ by making further disciples of all nations. They were to take what Jesus had given them and preach the good news of the kingdom, teaching people to obey what Jesus had taught them (Matthew 28:19–20). The evangelization of the world depended on their being fruitful (John 15:5, 8, 16). Thus the mission of God is contingent on the multiplication of ministry mentors.

9. RELATIONAL GROWTH

There is evidence of a progression in the mentoring relationship Jesus had with his disciples. Their relationship started with an invitation to follow and observe him. This relationship matured significantly and included participation in ministry, as is also illustrated by the principles of demonstration and delegation. Jesus increasingly revealed more of himself and his mission.

For example, the Gospel of Matthew highlights a turning point in Jesus' ministry wherein he took his disciples frequently into his confidence:

> *Then he ordered his disciples not to tell anyone that he was the Messiah.*
>
> *From that time on Jesus began to explain to his disciples that he must go to Jerusalem and suffer many things at the hands of the elders, the chief priests and the teachers of the law, and that he must be killed and on the third day be raised to life.*
>
> —Matthew 16:20–21

Eventually he was able to say,

> *No longer do I call you servants, for the servant does not know what his master is doing; but I have called you friends, for all that I have heard from my Father I have made known to you.*
>
> —John 15:15, ESV

This progression is indicative of the movement toward empowering his disciples to fulfill the ministry to which he had called them.

The implication for ministry mentoring is that the mentor needs to be conscious of the changing dynamic in his relationship with the mentee and adjust accordingly. For instance, mentees should receive expanded responsibilities and more autonomy. Also, both mentor and mentee should recognize that the relationship is moving toward a peer mentoring relationship.

10. PERSONAL ATTENTION

Another principle I want to mention is that of giving each mentee personal attention, as Jesus did with his disciples. In *Deep Mentoring*, Reese and Loane note that "Jesus *particularized* others throughout his earthly ministry—that is, he uniquely noticed them."[60]

Though Jesus employed what could be called a group mentoring model with the twelve, we also observe one-on-one moments of Jesus mentoring individuals. We see this especially in some descriptions of Jesus' interactions with Peter. Simon Peter's first recorded contact with Jesus results in the receiving of a new name and a new identity (John 1:35–42). Jesus later calls Peter away from his occupation as a fisherman to *"fish for people"* (Luke 5:1–10). Peter is commended for receiving a revelation of the true identity of Jesus, and shortly after that he is rebuked for trying to misdirect Jesus (Matthew 16:13–24). The miraculous provision of the temple tax teaches Peter that God is willing and able to provide for even the irritating needs of life such as paying taxes (Matthew 17:27). Jesus washes Peter's and the other apostles' feet, modelling the humility that his disciples should demonstrate (John 13:6–10). Jesus warns Peter that Satan has asked to sift him and then predicts that Peter will deny him (Luke 22:31–32 and Matthew 26:33–37). Jesus invites Peter, James, and John to pray with him in a critical hour but they are too tired to pray (Matthew 26:37–42). Peter tries to defend Jesus with the sword, but Jesus demonstrates that there are higher priorities than the defence of his person (John 18:10–11). Peter experiences the significant failure of denying the Lord Jesus (Matthew 26:33–37 and Luke 22:61). Later, Jesus restores and reinstates him (John 21:3–22).

---

60 Randy D. Reese and Robert Loane, *Deep Mentoring: Guiding Others on Their Leadership Journey* (Downers Grove, IL: IVP Books, 2012), 182.

These events provide a rich resource to understand how Jesus mentored an individual during a volatile ministry context. Most of these mentoring moments would have occurred within the hearing of the other disciples, and thus their value was multiplied for the group.

Jesus, as a mentor of the apostles during his earthly ministry, is an outstanding example of ministry mentoring in that he succeeded in transferring faith and ministry to the next generation. Just as Moses prepared Joshua to lead the people after Moses' death and David equipped Solomon to build the temple and rule Israel after David's death, so Jesus also empowered his apostles to make disciples of all nations after he ascended to heaven. This empowering included the promise of providing another mentor who would take his place.

THE HOLY SPIRIT AS MENTOR

A Greek word used in the New Testament that can be associated with the concept of mentoring is *paracletos*. The word is translated variously as helper, counsellor, or advocate. In the Gospel of John, Jesus gave the disciples this promise: *"And I will ask the Father, and he will give you another advocate to help you and be with you forever—the Spirit of truth"* (John 14:16–17a).[61] The word *paracletos* has a wide area of meaning which also includes consoler, encourager, and mediator.[62] It is used to describe the divine mentoring activity of the Holy Spirit, such as teaching, reminding, and guiding into all truth, in essence continuing the mentoring ministry of Jesus (John 14:26 and 15:13).

A theological consideration is that the activity of human mentoring resembles, but does not replace, the ministry of the Holy Spirit. However, the ministry mentor can be seen as the human agent through whom the Holy Spirit works, to help the mentee move toward his or her destiny in Christ.

Sometimes seminar participants have asked the question, "Why do we need human mentors if we have a divine mentor in the person of the Holy

---

61 See also John 14:26; 15:26; and 16:7.
62 Johannes P. Louw and Eugene Albert Nida, *Greek-English Lexicon of the New Testament: Based on Semantic Domains*, electronic edition of second edition, volume one (New York, NY: United Bible Societies, 1996), reference 12.19.

Spirit? Human mentors can mislead us, but the Holy Spirit will never lead us astray." I have answered that they need to understand there is always the possibility that their own heart, or perhaps even the devil, may lead them astray (Luke 22:31 and 2 Corinthians 11:3). Because those possibilities exist, a godly human mentor under the guidance of the Holy Spirit can provide necessary correction or affirmation when needed. The importance of a human mentor was illustrated at the beginning of this chapter in the story of Elizabeth's affirmation of Mary.

In the next chapter, we will look at other words and examples that are associated with ministry mentoring. In particular, we will examine the mentoring model that can be observed in the ministry of the apostle Paul.

QUESTIONS: FROM REFLECTION TO ACTION

1. Which aspects of Jesus' mentoring of his disciples stand out to you?
2. Of the ten principles mentioned, which do you think is the most difficult to incorporate into your ministry context? Why?
3. Which principle is the most countercultural in relation to your culture?
4. How can we distinguish between the divine mentoring activity of the Holy Spirit and that of a human mentor? How does the human mentor help us cooperate with the Holy Spirit?

Chapter Five

PAUL, THE SPIRITUAL PARENT MENTOR

A FASCINATING NEW TESTAMENT STORY WE RARELY HEAR ABOUT CONCERNS THE apostle Paul's mentoring of a runaway slave called Onesimus. In his letter to Philemon, Paul writes to his friend,

> *It is as none other than Paul—an old man and now also a prisoner of Christ Jesus—that I appeal to you for my son Onesimus, who became my son while I was in chains. Formerly he was useless to you, but now he has become useful both to you and to me.*
>
> *I am sending him—who is my very heart—back to you. I would have liked to keep him with me so that he could take your place in helping me while I am in chains for the gospel.*
>
> —Philemon 9–13

It appears that Onesimus had run away from his master, Philemon, and become connected with Paul. When he called Onesimus his son, he was using the term rabbis used to denote their disciples. In other words, Paul had become a mentor to him. We don't know how long the period of mentorship was, but now Onesimus, who was formerly useless, was transformed through his association with Paul and became useful for ministry.

In this story, we can also find hints of a mentoring relationship with Philemon. Paul, here as elsewhere, demonstrates the generous heart of a mentor. But before we look at Paul's mentoring model in greater depth, we need to consider Barnabas, whose name means "son of encouragement."

BARNABAS AS MENTOR

Barnabas stands out as a mentor in the New Testament because of his gift of encouragement and ability to see potential in others. However, he doesn't figure as prominently in the narrative as Peter and Paul. Raab and Clinton have done a study on Barnabas' mentoring activities and observed that

> Barnabas performed his first mentor-linking function when he sponsored Paul to the Jerusalem Christian leaders (Acts 9:23, 24). That Paul was accepted by the Jewish Christian leaders is evidence of the growth that had occurred in Barnabas' life. He was respected for his life, ministry, and judgment—all signs of spiritual authority. This divine contact with Paul was to be the key to God's expansion of Christianity to a Gentile world.[63]

As mentioned, ministry mentoring is fundamentally about the making of disciples for Christ. However, ministry mentoring also requires one to understand the importance of placing people in ministry according to what Clinton calls their respective "giftedness set"—namely, their natural abilities, acquired skills, and spiritual gifting.[64] This is for the purpose of being good stewards of the gifts God has given the church through its people. Barnabas as a mentor was an illustration of this principle when he facilitated the placing of Paul into the Antioch church where his giftedness set was a match for their needs.

Barnabas recognized the potential in Paul and sought him out to give him opportunities to grow, especially since the Antioch church was dynamic and now "sanctioned" by the Jerusalem church. This co-ministry with Paul accomplished three major things: it brought Paul into the mainstream of Christianity, it helped him develop his ministry gifts and status,

---

63 Laura Raab and J. Robert Clinton, *Barnabas, Encouraging Exhorter: A Study in Mentoring* (Altadena, CA: Barnabas Publishers, 1997), 12.

64 J. Robert Clinton and Dr. Richard Clinton, *Unlocking Your Giftedness: What Leaders Need to Know to Develop Themselves and Others* (Pasadena, CA: Barnabas Publishers, 1993), 40.

and it built up the Antioch church. This is evidenced by the term "Christians" first being used at Antioch and later by the mention of Paul being one of the teachers.[65]

Barnabas also had a mentoring role in John Mark's life. In fact, there came a point when he had to choose between Mark and Paul (Acts 15:36–39). The leadership role of the apostolic team had already fallen to Paul, so the mentoring role of Barnabas in Paul's ministry was concluded. Because of a dispute between them concerning Mark, they went in different directions and Barnabas took Mark under his wing. Mark was the future author of one of the gospels, thus Barnabas had a mentoring influence on two major biblical authors, Paul and Mark.[66]

NEW TESTAMENT MENTORING WORDS

The activity of ministry mentoring in the early church can be expressed this way:

> Mentoring or discipleship, as observed in the New Testament and early Christian writings was the work of one Christian helping another disciple or group of disciples grow in their knowledge and application of the teachings of Jesus and the Scriptures.[67]

Some keywords on the themes of discipleship are used in the New Testament to indicate how mentoring was understood in the time of Christ.[68] One of the more prominent ones is the word which we read in English as "disciple."[69] It includes the ideas of a follower, student, learner, and apprentice. Other people are also mentioned in Scripture as having a following of disciples, but primarily the word is used to denote a disciple of Christ.

---

65 Raab and Clinton, 28.
66 Other examples include Aquila and Pricilla's mentoring of Apollos (Acts 18:26) and the intergenerational example of Lois mentoring Eunice in the faith, who then mentored Timothy (2 Timothy 1:5).
67 Smither, 12.
68 These have been highlighted by Smither, 4–11.
69 In Greek, *mathetes*.

When the apostles were instructed to make disciples of all nations, they understood that they were to make disciples of Christ, not their own disciples (Matthew 28:19). Ministry mentoring includes disciple-making, but it also involves equipping others for contextual ministry (Ephesians 4:12).

Among other things, Jesus was called a teacher who had a following of disciples.[70] It was in this role that he mentored and trained his disciples. This kind of teacher-disciple relationship was prevalent in the Middle Eastern culture of New Testament times, and Jesus adapted this form of transferring knowledge and skills for the purposes of the kingdom.

The authoritative learning content in this teacher-disciple relationship was "sound teaching."[71] This teaching is based on the "Scriptures" or "sacred writings" which became the foundation of all discipleship training and ministry mentoring.[72] Jesus' life and ministry were a fulfilment of the Old Testament scriptures and his teaching flowed out of the same scriptures. In his final command to the apostles, he said, *"Make disciples of all nations... teaching them to observe all that I have commanded you"* (Matthew 28:19–20, ESV). The early church *"devoted themselves to the apostles' teaching"* (Acts 2:42, ESV). The apostle Paul, in giving Titus instructions for a spiritual leader in the church, said, *"He must hold firm to the trustworthy word as taught, so that he may be able to give instruction in sound doctrine and also to rebuke those who contradict it"* (Titus 1:9, ESV). Thus, sound teaching founded in Scripture became a strong feature in the mentoring process of the early church. The apostle Paul, a ministry mentor to Timothy, emphasizes the importance of Scripture as a learning and equipping resource:

> *But as for you, continue in what you have learned and have firmly believed, knowing from whom you learned it and how from childhood you have been acquainted with the sacred writings, which are able to make you wise for salvation through faith in Christ Jesus. All Scripture is breathed out by God and profitable for teaching, for reproof, for correction, and for*

---

70   In Greek, *didaskalos*. The Aramaic word was *rabbi*.
71   In Greek, *hygiainouse didaskalia*, sometimes translated as "sound doctrine."
72   In Greek, *graphai* for "scriptures" and *hiera grammata* for "sacred writings."

training in righteousness, that the man of God may be complete, equipped for every good work.
—2 Timothy 3:14–17, ESV

To explicitly connect these New Testament words with our definition of ministry mentoring, consider the following:

- The disciple is the *mentee*.
- The teacher is the guiding *mentor* in the *learning relationship*.
- The sound teaching based on Scripture or the sacred writings is the substance and content which informs the *critical growth pathways*.

PAUL AS MENTOR

We see Jesus as the ultimate New Testament example of a mentor. However, another significant example is the apostle Paul. He was trained at the feet of Gamaliel using traditional Jewish methods that included the mentoring relationship between a rabbi and his disciple (Acts 22:3). As mentioned, he was also mentored by Barnabas. Paul demonstrated great passion in his mentoring of Timothy, Titus, Onesimus, and others in his apostolic teams. The book of Acts and the letters of Paul, particularly the pastoral epistles, include examples of his mentoring practices. We see this best in his letters to Timothy.

Mentoring Timothy

In his two letters to Timothy, Paul offers advice and counsel interspersed with instructions for the churches he was overseeing. He was relating to Timothy as a ministry mentor. These letters had the function of building up Timothy as a minister, while at the same time empowering Timothy with delegated apostolic authority so that he could fulfill his ministry responsibilities. These letters, while addressed to Timothy personally, were also read publicly so that the churches could know that the things Timothy taught them were based on apostolic authority.

Their mentoring relationship started as they ministered together in the planting of several churches in Asia Minor (Acts 16:1–3). The relationship progressed to the level where Paul delegated, released, and empowered Timothy into a particular ministry context.

In the letters to Timothy, Paul reminds him of Timothy's divine calling and the content of Paul's teaching.[73] He encourages the young man to stay on task as a teacher and example.[74] Paul advises him about how to relate appropriately to the people in his spiritual care (1 Timothy 5:1–2). Paul also encourages him to persevere in the face of worldly distractions (1 Timothy 6:11–12, 20–21).

Paul's Benevolent Parenting Analogy

In some of Paul's letters to the churches, he uses the analogy of a spiritual parent to describe how he related to the people in the churches he founded.[75] He viewed them as his spiritual children. On several occasions, he also used the father-son analogy when speaking of his relationship with Timothy.[76]

I highlight the analogy of spiritual fathering and mothering as a part of the ministry mentoring model of this book. Of particular interest here is the apostle Paul's sacrificial attitude for the benefit of his spiritual children that he modelled and expressed: *"So I will very gladly spend for you everything I have and expend myself as well"* (2 Corinthians 12:15a). He similarly expressed this sentiment after the Galatian church experienced a spiritual setback: *"My dear children, for whom I am again in the pains of childbirth until Christ is formed in you"* (Galatians 4:19).

His parenting language also included both discipline and nurturance. In addressing the church in Corinth, he writes, *"What do you prefer? Shall I come to you with a rod of discipline, or shall I come in love and with a gentle spirit?"* (1 Corinthians 4:21) The mentor-disciple relationships in the New Testament and early church included rigorous discipline which was tempered

---

73 1 Timothy 1:18–19a; 2 Timothy 1:6; 1 Timothy 4:6–8; 2 Timothy 2:15–16; and 3:14–15.
74 1 Timothy 4:11–16; 2 Timothy 2:1–3; 2:22–23; and 4:2.
75 1 Corinthians 4:14–18; 2 Corinthians 6:11–13; 12:14–15; Galatians. 4:19; and 1 Thessalonians 2:7–12.
76 1 Corinthians 4:17; Philippians 2:22; 1 Timothy 1:2, 18; and 2 Timothy 2:1.

by grace. Jesus set high standards for his disciples, but he also demonstrated patience while they grew under his mentorship. Though there was an element of power and authority in the relationship, this power was never used inappropriately. The relationship developed from master-servant and teacher-student to friendship. The early church fathers also understood and practiced "a balance between fatherly tenderness and spiritual authority."[77] This is the same dynamic that is expressed in the apostle Paul's analogy of a *benevolent parent*.

Another aspect of Paul's spiritual parenting or mentoring is his transparent style of relating. For instance, he invites his spiritual children to emulate him: *"Be imitators of me, as I am of Christ"* (1 Corinthians 11:1, ESV).[78] The mentorship included both modelling of ministry and participation in ministry. We have already seen this principle in Jesus' mentoring principles of demonstration and delegation. Paul did the same with his apostolic teams, which included Timothy, Titus, Epaphras, Epaphroditus, and others over the course of his ministry.[79]

This style of relating as an exemplary model is similarly expressed by the apostle Peter as he instructs leaders using the ministry leadership analogy of shepherding a flock:

> *Be shepherds of God's flock that is under your care, watching over them— not because you must, but because you are willing, as God wants you to be; not pursuing dishonest gain, but eager to serve; not lording it over those entrusted to you, but being examples to the flock.*
>
> —1 Peter 5:2–3

Whether we use the analogy of parenting or shepherding, the mentor's relationship with the mentee is a sacred trust that demonstrates concern for the well-being of the mentee and recognizes the profound influence a mentor can have as an example that points toward Christ. The implications

---

77   Smither, 68.
78   See also 1 Corinthians 4:16; Philippians 3:17; 1 Thessalonians 1:6–7; and 2 Thessalonians 3:7–8.
79   1 Timothy 3:14; 4;6–16; Titus 1:5; Colossians 4:12–13; and Philippians 2:19–30.

are that in a ministry mentoring relationship, the mentor must embrace the attitude of a parent who focuses primarily on the well-being of the mentee. The mentor applies appropriate discipline when necessary and provides nurturing care as required. At the same time, he or she remains transparent as an example of how to live and work.

When considering the parenting analogy concerning ministry mentoring, it cannot be assumed that all parenting practices that have been experienced by children are right or even helpful. Nor have all parents been good examples for their children. It is for this reason that we use the term *benevolent parent*. This expression helps to highlight the altruistic aspects of parenting attitudes and behaviours which we would require of good mentors toward their mentees in a ministry mentoring relationship. Included in that term is the appropriate balance of gracious nurturance and constructive discipline.

Generativity of Ministry

As has been seen in other biblical examples of ministry mentoring, Paul was similarly concerned about the generativity of ministry. He understood the priority of transferring faith from one generation to another. He expressed this to Timothy, his mentee, toward the end of his life:

> *What you heard from me, keep as the pattern of sound teaching, with faith and love in Christ Jesus. Guard the good deposit that was entrusted to you—guard it with the help of the Holy Spirit who lives in us.*
> —2 Timothy 1:13–14

He continues on this theme later in the same letter: *"And the things you have heard me say in the presence of many witnesses entrust to reliable people who will also be qualified to teach others"* (2 Timothy 2:2).

Resourcing

Even after releasing the mentee into ministry, an aspect of the mentoring relationship continues through the ongoing resourcing of spiritual leaders.

This relationship, however, takes on a different form in which the disciple still values and welcomes the mentor's input but is no longer dependent on the mentor. One way in which this occurred in the early church was through the writing of letters. Paul wrote letters that resourced Timothy and Titus; at least one of the letters was written from prison while Paul awaited execution.

As the apostle Paul reflected on his work among the church people in Philippi, he reminded them of God's continuing activity among them: *"he who began a good work in you will carry it on to completion until the day of Christ Jesus"* (Philippians 1:6).

SUMMARIZING BIBLICAL MENTORING INSIGHTS

In these last three chapters, we have considered a biblical and theological basis for ministry mentoring. It started with looking at God's purposeful partnership with humankind. We highlighted biblical examples of mentoring from both testaments, demonstrating that mentoring helped to equip leaders and transfer faith and leadership skills from one generation to another. We described Jesus' model of leadership regarding intentional ministry mentoring. The mentoring activity of the Holy Spirit was briefly considered as potentially being mediated through a human mentor. We discussed New Testament terms which inform a theology of mentoring, as well as the apostle Paul's mentoring analogy of a benevolent parent.

The survey of mentoring stories and examples in the Bible point us toward some ministry mentoring principles. They contribute to our understanding of ministry mentoring. The insights gained from them provide the spiritual foundations and rationale for the best practices of ministry mentoring. In the remaining chapters, we will learn some of those best practices.

QUESTIONS: FROM REFLECTION TO ACTION

1. What are some of the things a person like Barnabas might think as he interacts with people like Paul and Mark? To what degree is that a mindset you could embrace?
2. What are some things that stand out to you in the relationship between Paul and Timothy?
3. Why is Scripture so important to the ministry mentor?
4. What would a benevolent parent mentoring model look like in your context? What can be embraced easily and what would be the most difficult to incorporate?
5. What steps would you need to take in your ministry to ensure that mentoring occurs to the fourth generation, as described in 2 Timothy 2:2?

Part II
MINISTRY MENTORING IN PRACTICE

Chapter Six

WHAT MENTORS DO—MENTORING ACTIVITIES

TO BE A CARPENTER, YOU NEED TO KNOW HOW TO DO SEVERAL THINGS. For example, you need to know how to hammer nails and fasten things together with screws. You need to be able to measure, cut, plane, and sand wood. For each of those tasks, you need to use the appropriate tool. You do not use a hammer to drive screws into wood. You do not use sandpaper to reduce the length of a board by an inch. Use a saw. It's quicker.

Carpenters who go into business for themselves also acquire additional skills, such as estimating projects, preparing invoices, and dealing with customers. They may also hire and train employees. Ministry mentoring is a little like that. You have the ministry skills you use on a regular basis, but when you want to be a mentor, you need to acquire another set of skills. Engaging in mentoring activities and acquiring the necessary skills will augment your ministry and broaden your impact as you advance the kingdom of God.

In this chapter, we want to describe some of the primary activities of a mentor and suggest the potential roles of a mentor. This is to provide a framework for an intentional mentoring relationship. In actual practice, what the mentor does flows out of who the mentor is, but it is helpful to understand first what the mentor does so that the mentor can know who he or she needs to become and why.

The various activities that relate to mentorship will be explained under separate headings.[80] These are best seen as tools in a toolbox, each one

---

80 The material in chapters six and seven adapts some of the concepts presented in Johnson and Ridley, 1–72.

ready to use at appropriate times in the mentoring relationship. Every situation and context will require the mentor to adapt and adjust what they do, depending on the ability and availability of the mentor, the needs and commitment of the mentees, as well as the boundaries of the culture and specific contexts.

INTENTIONAL ENGAGEMENT—SELECTION OF THE MENTEE

When we speak of mentee selection, we envision an intentional, ongoing mentoring relationship which assumes many meetings over a timespan of months or possibly years.[81] We have seen in Chapter Four that Jesus intentionally and carefully selected those disciples with whom he would spend more time. Mentoring relationships take time to build, so the mentor will want to invest her time wisely. Jesus had prayed all night before he chose the twelve (Luke 6:12–13). Mentors will do well to pray, asking God for wisdom to choose those with whom they should be in a mentoring relationship. We cannot mentor everyone, so we need to ask how many we can handle in our current situations.

Some questions the mentor asks of him or herself about prospective mentees in the selection process include:

- Who is willing to be mentored?
- How well do you fit together regarding personality?
- Why do you want to mentor a particular person? What are your motives?
- What is best for the person being mentored and what is best for the kingdom?
- What are your expectations in the relationship?
- What are the expectations of the mentee in the relationship?

As the mentor deliberates whether or not to begin a mentoring relationship, there are other things to discern which relate specifically to the

---

[81] Mentee selection may not be a primary concern in casual mentoring encounters with occasional mentees.

mentee. The mentor will want to determine whether the mentee shows evidence of being called to the ministry to which they are aspiring and seeking to be mentored in. Further, the mentor will want to determine whether the mentee has a willing and teachable spirit. Failing to discern correctly on these points can lead to the wasting of valuable time on an individual who is clearly not called or willing, even though they appear to be gifted.

Mentee selection in various ministry contexts can happen in three ways:

- The mentee requests to be mentored by a particular mentor.
- The mentor seeks out and selects the mentee directly.
- The mentor and mentee are assigned to each other by the organization in which they serve.

Whichever way it happens, the mentor finally needs to accept or decline the mentoring responsibility according to the criteria already mentioned and how they sense the Spirit of God is directing them at the time.

THE ISSUE OF AVAILABILITY

Another important factor to consider when selecting a mentee is how much time the mentor will be able to give to the relationship. A mentor needs to be available to the mentee and schedule adequate time to invest in them. Developing a relationship in which healthy mentoring occurs takes a lot of time, particularly in the beginning when a framework of the relationship is worked out. At this point, matters can be discussed and agreements made to manage expectations. The frequency of meetings, the length of sessions, and the duration of the formal mentorship can all be considered at the beginning of the relationship and be renegotiated as necessary.

There may be times when the mentor wants to include the mentee in their ministry schedule to be together in diverse settings for building a relationship and modelling behaviours and attitudes as they emerge. There is also much value in spending time in non-ministry settings, for the same reasons. There are likely to be occasions for spontaneous, unscheduled, or emergency connecting. The mentor needs to be prepared for the impact that a mentoring relationship will have on her time. A ministry mentoring relationship needs to be embraced as an integral part of ministry once a commitment is made to mentor someone. Ultimately, given all the other responsibilities in his or her life, the mentor needs to make a choice to take on the mentoring responsibilities. Of course, the actual time that mentoring takes will depend on what the mentoring agreement indicates. For example, the agreement may be to meet for an hour on a monthly basis or be as time-intensive as a daily engagement in ministry contexts. We will look at mentoring agreements in more detail in Chapter Ten.

KNOWING THE MENTEE

The focus of a mentoring relationship is on the mentees. For that reason, mentors will do well to take the time and effort to get to know well the persons being mentored. This will enable the mentor to fine-tune their approach concerning the mentees' uniqueness as an individual and also help them move toward greater self-awareness in the various aspects of their life and ministry. For instance, mentors should observe and answer these questions about their mentees:

- What are their gifts and abilities?
- What are their fears?
- What is their pain?
- What are their passions?
- What is the best way of helping them align their priorities and reach their potential?[82]

---

82   David A. Stoddard and Robert Tamasy, *The Heart of Mentoring: Ten Proven Principles for Developing People to Their Fullest Potential*, Kindle edition (Colorado Springs, CO: NavPress, 2003), 11.

Self-awareness of the mentee is dealt with in more detail in Chapter Eight. Also, you the mentor may continually ask these questions about your mentee as the relationship progresses:

- How far have they advanced since you last saw them?
- What are indicators of their eagerness to grow?
- What input is God calling you to have in their lives at this time?

As you mentor someone, always ask, "What is God doing in this person's life and how can I cooperate with what he is doing?" As the mentor gets to know the mentee, the mentor must be careful not to make unwarranted assumptions about the mentee. A wrong assumption, particularly at the beginning of a relationship, can set the mentoring relationship seriously off course. The discussion in Chapter Eight will guide the mentor in getting to know the mentee sufficiently to be of help to him.

Identify and Call out the Gifts

As the mentor gets to know the mentee, a picture emerges of the potential that exists within them. It is the mentor's responsibility to call that potential out into behavioural reality.

The mentor needs to work with what is within the mentee, not try to squeeze something out of the mentee that is not already there in seed form. Every mentee is unique, possessing different gifts, abilities, experiences, and passions. The mentor needs to discern what those are and reinforce them. The mentee may not always be aware of them, so the mentor needs to help identify those strengths and encourage their development. The mentor should be quick to acknowledge the appropriate use of the mentee's gifts and abilities and celebrate growth with them in those areas.

The Art of Listening Well

Listening is an important skill that helps the mentor get to know the mentee. We cannot assume that we are all good listeners, but we can all learn to listen better.

An important starting point to listening well is to understand what it means to be fully present to the mentee. A good mentor gives his full attention to what the mentee says and does. All potential distractions are removed (such as mobile phones) and other work is set aside. The mentor should allow the mentee to finish speaking their thoughts without interrupting. The mentor should give nonverbal cues that demonstrate interest and follow up with relevant questions.

Some active listening techniques can be used, such as restating ("I heard you say… did I hear you correctly?") and probing ("Can you tell me more about that…? What do you think happened? Why?") The mentor should also watch for nonverbal clues and take note of what is not said.

The mentor needs to guard against assuming anything about the mentee. The mentee needs to be adequately heard and understood before moving on to problem-solving. One way to make sure the mentor has listened well is for him or her to summarize what was said and to have the mentee acknowledge that the summary correctly represents what was said.

Asking Good Questions

Listening well in a mentoring conversation is often facilitated by asking the right kinds of questions. There are different types of questions, and the mentor will do well to be aware of them and know when to ask them. For instance, some questions elicit information, such as "What happened? Who did what?" Other questions lead to learning conversations, such as "Why do you think that happened?" Some questions invite personal reflection, such as "How did that make you feel?" Questions that dig deeper may ask, "What else has not yet been considered?" A question leading to greater self-awareness may ask something like this: "What do you think made you do that at that time?" A question that helps to clarify may ask, "What do you mean by that?"

In a mentoring or coaching conversation, there is also a time to stop asking questions and identify the insights gained, and to help the mentee integrate those into their life and ministry. Chapter Nine, which deals with the mentoring agenda, explains this kind of engagement in more detail and proposes ways of designing critical growth pathways for the mentoring relationship.

AFFIRMATION AND ENCOURAGEMENT

Affirming and encouraging are the most critical of mentoring activities. Affirmation relates to what already is. When things get difficult, mentees need to be reminded of their worth, who they are, and what they have already achieved. When mentors tell them of this, they affirm them. From a spiritual perspective, affirmation is the mentor expressing faith and confidence in the mentee as the person God meant them to be, and also reminding them of what God has already helped them to accomplish.

Encouragement relates to what has yet to be accomplished. The mentee may face an overwhelming task or need emotional support, especially when they face adverse circumstances and uncooperative people. Negative feedback, wherever it comes from, sticks more readily and leads to discouragement, so an increase in encouragement is always welcome. Even talented people need to be encouraged from time to time. Encouraging words and actions can help them see things more positively. It has been suggested that "it takes five positive comments to offset the impact of a single negative one."[83]

As for verbal praise, some require more and others are uncomfortable with too much. Let it always be sincere. Offer enough to make a difference, but not so much that it loses value or becomes addictive. Find different ways to express praise. For instance, a note in a card or email which specifically states what they did well and how you feel about it. Another powerful way to express praise, when appropriate, is to speak it in the hearing of others who will celebrate the mentee's achievements with you.

---

83 Tony Schwartz, Jean Gomes, and Catherine McCarthy, *Be Excellent at Anything: The Four Keys to Transforming the Way We Work and Live*, Kindle edition (New York: Free Press, 2010), 168.

Affirm the Heart of the Dream

A young ministry leader may share with his mentor grand visions and dreams concerning future ministry plans and expectations. Having the benefit of more experience, the mentor may know that some of these things are not realistic. A skilled mentor will know how to affirm the heart out of which the dream flows while at the same time gently suggest more realistic scenarios and help the mentee to see real limitations, thus reducing the scope of the vision to something that is achievable and significant.

Steve Saccone, author of *Protégé* and founder of a global leadership program at Mosaic Church in Los Angeles, offers this mentoring tip: "When a protégé takes a risk, steps out in courage, or initiates, make sure you affirm their proactivity... Celebrate the right kind of risks even if the desired outcome doesn't happen."[84]

Stimulate Growth with Challenging Assignments

During the mentoring relationship, the mentor wants to see the mentees expand their capacity for ministry. One of the ways to do this is to give them assignments that challenge and stretch them. They should not be given jobs that are so far beyond their ability that they fail and become discouraged. Neither should the assignments be so easy that they become complacent and lose interest.

Assignments should be based on the area of the mentees' actual ministry, representing where they need to grow. It is best when such an assignment is something mentees themselves design or at least participate in designing. As they launch into their assignments, the mentor will help them to overcome their fears by encouraging them along the way. After the task is completed, good mentors will take the time to debrief so they can provide correction and encouragement.

Provide Correction

There are two general areas in which correction may be required. One relates to Christian behaviour and character issues, and the other relates to

---

[84] Steve Saccone and Cheri Saccone, *Protégé: Developing Your Next Generation of Church Leaders* (Downers Grove, IL: IVP Books, 2012), 227.

skill development issues. Since ministry mentoring as defined in this book refers to life and ministry, both of these areas are in view.

Correction needs to be balanced with affirmation. For instance, it is important to deal with behaviours that are unethical, improper, ungodly, and sinful. We cannot affirm such ways, but we need to reaffirm the identity in Christ of the mentee who has behaved beneath their Christian calling. If they have been caught in a lie, the mentor does not label them a liar. Rather, the mentor will say something that reflects this kind of thinking: "You are a follower of Christ; followers of Christ do not lie, yet in this instance you have lied. What do you think you need to do to bring your behaviour back into alignment with your identity?" This both corrects the mentee's behaviour while affirming them as a person.

In the case of dealing with mistakes, failures, and errors in judgment, the wise mentor will have created a relational environment and context that is generally affirming of the mentee's ministry skills. Then, when it becomes necessary to correct the mentee for doing something wrong, a simple corrective debriefing will usually suffice.

Once, when I had done something unwise, my mentor (who also happened to be my ministry supervisor) confronted me. He only said, "Don't ever do that again!" Because he was generally affirming of my ministry, it was not difficult to receive that simple rebuke, and yes, I got the point and never repeated that behaviour.

Sometimes the correction can take the form of a longer debriefing, and the unwise behaviour can be analyzed along these lines: "Do you know what you did wrong? Do you understand why it is wrong? What would a more appropriate and wise approach or behaviour have been in this case?" Again, this is done in an environment of ongoing affirmation and encouragement. This is the approach the apostle Paul took in his letters to the churches: first commendation, then correction, followed by instruction and encouragement.

Correction does not need to be overly negative and judgmental in a way that discourages. Rather, correction is more effective when it is framed with grace that shows the way forward. In most cases, it is best to provide correction away from the ears of others. Publicly shaming the mentee is usually not helpful.

Narrate Growth and Development

As a mentor, it is useful from time to time to help mentees gain a broader perspective about their development. This is done by enabling them to see what specific progress they have made over time. It often helps to remind them of the starting point, such as the beginning of the mentoring relationship, and identify areas where there is evidence of personal growth and fruitfulness in ministry. The mentee should then be encouraged to determine their current situation and direction of movement.

Finally, the mentor can invite them to think of the preferred future as a reasonable possibility based on the evidence of any forward movement they have experienced. An example statement could be: "I remember when you used to [be like this]; now you [are like this]; soon you will progress to [be like this]."

Sometimes the mentee may not be aware of their progress until you describe it to them. This type of reflection can be an encouragement to the mentee in their growth, particularly in seasons of discouragement.

Nurture Creativity

The mentee is a unique individual who may have some innovative approaches to ministry. However, conventional systems and the people who are comfortable with the status quo have a way of stifling creativity. A mentoring relationship provides a safe place and an opportunity for the mentee to talk about new ideas. The mentor can be a sounding board for these ideas, and in fact should encourage discussion about them and how these may be integrated into the ministry context. The mentor may be able to provide the wisdom required to actually implement these ideas in the best way. This is the kind of discussion where the mentor can also learn new things and participate in potentially exciting endeavours.

THE POTENTIAL ROLES OF A MENTOR

The mentor may have the opportunity to play various roles in the life of the mentee depending on their learning need at any given time, such as teacher, coach, counsellor, or spiritual director. In playing these roles, the mentor doesn't necessarily replace other skilled individuals but may occasionally engage the mentee in those particular modes. The mentor, of course, may have the skills to do this and be able to serve the mentee well. Where skills are lacking, limitations should be acknowledged, and the mentor may do better to refer the mentee to someone with the necessary expertise and experience. Often the mentee will be able to find the necessary help when the mentor suggests the need. That being said, the mentor can also be on a journey to grow in some of these skills.

The art of mentoring is to discern the right times to engage the mentee in these different roles.

Mentor as Teacher

As a teacher, the mentor will teach the mentees what they need to know and give specific instruction when necessary. If the mentor is not sufficiently knowledgeable in a particular field, he or she can help them find someone else who is or point them to some resource materials that will assist them. In the teaching role, the mentor provides resources by leading the mentee to the right books, courses, and other experts and offers the opportunity to process with the mentee the learning that occurs through those resources.

Just as a teacher gives homework to help a student grow and develop, mentors provide assignments to mentees which stretch them toward greater capacity. They make the tasks difficult enough to challenge them, but not so demanding that the mentees become overwhelmed lest they become discouraged. As they launch out on an assignment, mentors will help them overcome fears. While the mentee works on the task, the mentor will encourage them as necessary. After completion, the mentor should provide an opportunity to discuss how it went and offer feedback, including correction if required.

Mentor as Coach

Mentors should learn some basic coaching skills and have an understanding of how a coaching conversation goes. Good coaching conversations will facilitate the mentee's ability to maintain ownership of their own learning. The mentor should coach them through ministry activities as they need it.

If you are in a position to do so, find opportunities to let the mentees try a variety of ministry activities which require increasing levels of competence, and then coach them through these activities until they gain confidence.

Mentor as Counsellor

Sometimes the mentor plays the role of counsellor. As such, it is important to have a relationship in which you can be open to discussing all issues of life and ministry.

Active listening is an important counselling skill, and it means listening carefully and then reflecting back to the individual what they have said using your own words. If they confirm your interpretation of their words, then you have heard them, and they know it. Pay attention to the emotion in their voice. It is also important to observe their body language as you hear them express themselves. The mentor as counsellor knows the wisdom of listening at all levels before answering. A biblical proverb highlights the importance of this principle: *"To answer before listening—that is folly and shame"* (Proverbs 18:13).

Help them to understand their feelings by asking appropriate questions such as "When you say… what are you feeling?" and "Why do you think you are feeling like this?" If it's an issue of making decisions, help them to see the full range of alternatives. Be prepared to offer wise counsel but recognize your limitations as a mentor. Some issues may be outside your expertise and experience. Do not hesitate to help your mentee find the help they need elsewhere.

Mentor as Spiritual Director

There may be times when the mentee needs help to hear God's voice and discern spiritual direction. The mentor will need to be particularly sensitive to what the Holy Spirit is doing in the life of the mentee and help him or her to pay attention to the subtle working of the Spirit. At these times, prayer for and with the mentee is crucial, as well as helping them to ask the right kind of questions in their devotional life and prayer times. Pointing them to relevant passages of Scripture and suggesting different types of spiritual discipline will also be helpful.

This is not necessarily the time for a personal prophetic word, even though the mentor may have a strong sense of direction on behalf of the mentee. For mentees to develop spiritual maturity, it is best to allow them to discover for themselves what God is saying. The role of the mentor as a spiritual director is simply to nudge them in the direction where they are most likely to discover what they need.

Mentor as Supervisor

In many mentoring contexts, the mentor also has a supervisory role in relationship to the mentee. In other words, the same person helping the mentee in their personal development also must have the objectives of the organization in view. This can sometimes lead to role confusion, reducing the openness that is required in a healthy mentoring relationship.

For example, the same person who helps the mentee may also be the one who can "fire" them. While this may not be ideal, it can be workable if the two roles are clearly defined and understood. On the one hand, there will be times when the supervisory relationship takes precedence and the focus rests on the organization's work objectives. On the other hand, there will be times when the mentoring relationship comes to the forefront, and the focus rests on the development of the mentee. Imagine wearing "the boss hat" and "the mentoring hat"—two hats worn by the same person at different times. Sometimes it may be helpful for the mentor to state which hat he or she is wearing, especially when there may be some ambiguity. This scenario is discussed further in Chapter Twelve.

Mentor as Expert

It should be safe to assume that the mentor is the expert in the relationship—at least in the specific areas in which the mentee wants to increase their learning. The experience of the mentor is what the mentee wants to tap into, and the mentor helps the mentee get onto a pathway of learning that will assist them in gaining the expertise they require. In this role, the mentor is both a teacher and a model. However, the highly effective mentor will guide mentees to develop their own approach to the expertise they seek, according to the unique abilities of each mentee.

Mentor as Model

Often the mentee is attracted to the mentor because of the mentor's skill, characteristics, and approach to ministry. The mentee wants to emulate those things and hopes that some of those qualities rub off in the mentoring relationship. The mentee wants to observe the mentor.

So the mentor is, in this instance, a model or example to be followed. The mentor allows himself to be observed in different ministry contexts and provides an opportunity to discuss how and why he did certain things. The mentee learns thereby how he can also do those things and adopt the right attitude and stance in a variety of ministry and life situations.

Mentor as Sage

Sometimes mentors are simply seen as wise older people with life experience who give advice when asked. We know that a mentor does more than that. In fact, a highly effective mentor will resist giving advice too quickly. Rather, the mentor invites the mentee on a journey of discovery of insight through the various activities we have discussed so far.

But that does not mean that the mentor will never give advice. At the end of the process of discovery, the mentee will still want to hear some good advice from the mentor. The mentee will trust the mentor's wisdom and should at certain times have the benefit of hearing that wisdom in the form of advice.

In this chapter, we have identified some of the things a mentor does and some of the roles a mentor plays. In the next chapter, we will discuss the kind of person a mentor needs to be in order to be effective.

QUESTIONS: FROM REFLECTION TO ACTION

1. What skills do you currently have that will work well in a mentoring relationship?
2. What mentoring skills do you need to cultivate to be a better mentor?
3. When you have mentored, what roles have you played?
4. Which role do you think you will try to use more of after reading this chapter?
5. What will you do differently next time you mentor someone?

Chapter Seven

WHO MENTORS ARE—MENTORING ATTITUDE

MENTORS KNOW THAT IN A SENSE THEY ARE GIVING THEMSELVES AWAY. This speaks to the generous spirit and attitude that mentoring inevitably requires. Mentors must always be willing to help, even it costs something in terms of time, money, and energy. Mentoring is not for those who are interested only in their own development and advancement. The mentor is basically unselfish and doesn't hold back what will help his or her mentee.

In almost every activity, what we do and how we function flows out of who we are. In this part of the book, we want to focus on the heart of the mentor. Jesus said, *"The good person out of the good treasure of his heart produces good, and the evil person out of his evil treasure produces evil, for out of the abundance of the heart his mouth speaks"* (Luke 6:45, ESV). An Old Testament proverb reads, *"Above all else, guard your heart, for everything you do flows from it"* (Proverbs 4:23). We may acquire mentoring competencies and understand how mentoring is supposed to work, but if we fail to pay attention to our heart, character, and attitude, we are unlikely to be effective.

WHAT A MINISTRY MENTOR VALUES

The philosophy of ministry of a mentor will reflect the importance of leadership development. Equipping those with emerging leadership qualities in the church will be high on the list of the mentor's priorities. She understands that if the church neglects to equip the next generation of leaders, its mission will suffer setbacks. She recognizes the value of each potential leader and the gifts they bring to the ministry. She knows that each one must relate to someone who will help them find their place in ministry.

Advancing the Kingdom of God through Mentoring

A primary value for mentors is participating in serving the purposes of God in our generation (Acts 13:36). When we align ourselves with the rule of God, his kingdom advances in and through our lives. And to the degree that we help others align themselves with the rule of God, the effect is multiplied and our impact as Christian ministers serves to advance the kingdom of God even more. When the Holy Spirit draws our attention to his work in the life of an emerging minister and invites us to facilitate that work, it is an opportunity to make a difference in that person for the sake of the kingdom. One of the greatest joys of a mentor is seeing someone they have been able to influence make their own impact in serving the purposes of God.

Always a Learner

The mentor never graduates from being a disciple. In that spirit, Augustine is quoted as saying, "For you I am a bishop, with you I am a Christian."[85] This is similar to the attitude of the apostle Paul, who never felt that he had arrived: *"Not that I have already obtained all this, or have already arrived at my goal, but I press on to take hold of that for which Christ Jesus took hold of me"* (Philippians 3:12).

Jesus, though he was sinless, modelled a dependence on God, taking "the posture of a disciple."[86] Even the other apostles, in what can be considered peer mentoring relationships, practiced mutual submission. For example, the apostle Peter received correction from the apostle Paul in the crucial matter of Jews eating with Gentiles (Galatians 2:11–14 and 2 Peter 3:15–16). The early church also constantly engaged each other in discussions about Scripture in the spirit of being simultaneously teachers and learners together.

---

85 Smither, 16.
86 Ibid., 15.

A Standard of Excellence

In an intentional mentoring relationship, it is important for the mentor to have a value of excellence in ministry. Mentors can only set as high a standard for their mentees as they have set for themselves, both in character and ministry skills. Striving for excellence is highly desirable in a mentoring relationship—to be the best we can be with what we have been given in ability and opportunity. However, it is important that excellence not be confused with perfection. Perfection is not possible for most people, but everyone can have a spirit of excellence. Since excellence rejoices in progress, what the mentor is looking for in the mentee is a robust movement in the right direction:

- Are they moving toward God's best for them or away from it?
- Are they passionate about doing the best they can or only doing what it takes to get by?
- Have they advanced in their character and skill development, or have they plateaued?
- Is there evidence of increasing maturity, or have they regressed?

EMBRACE YOUR MENTORING STYLE

Mentors do not need to be perfect for mentees to learn from them. An astute mentee can learn from us even if we don't have all the characteristics that might be expected of an ideal mentor.

In a study, 1,011 mentees were asked to describe the personal characteristics of their mentors. Eight dimensions emerged: authenticity, nurturance, approachability, competence, inspiration, conscientious, hardworking, and volatility.[87]

Volatility is one of the characteristics usually not included in mentoring descriptions, yet it apparently has some significance:

---

87 Ann Darwin, "Characteristics Ascribed to Mentors by Their Protégés," in *The Situational Mentor: An International Review of Competencies and Capabilities in Mentoring*, ed. David Clutterbuck and Gill Lane (Burlington, VT: Gower, 2004), 30–1.

> Protégés who attributed high Volatility scores to their mentors were able to observe the mentor's behavior, utilize the 'best' (those actions which teach the learner how to progress forward in an organization) and discard the worst... A good mentor may be a competent person with major flaws so that one can learn what to do and what not to do at the same time.[88]

It is possible then for mentoring experiences to be negative at one level, yet mentees can discern in themselves positive outcomes on another level. However, it is generally expected that mentors exude a warm and friendly attitude toward their mentees, which strengthens the learning relationship.

The multidimensional profiles that emerged in the study also determined that there are different styles of mentoring. Some mentors may be more people-oriented, so they focus on the needs of the mentee. They tend to be more nurturing, approachable, and authentic. Others may be more task-oriented, so they focus on what needs to get done in each context. They may be inspirational, push for hard work, and have volatile tendencies.

Regarding the individuals in the study, the insights can help a mentor to be aware of the mentoring style to which she gravitates as she considers the needs of her mentee. Sometimes the mentee needs a season of nurturing and healing, but for mentees to become useful in their roles in the organization or community, they may need to experience a more direct approach that challenges them to get on with the job. If a mentor does not match the needs of her mentee, one option is to refer the mentee to a more appropriate mentor. Another possibility is to adapt her mentoring style between the polarities of people-orientation and task-orientation, according to the mentee's needs, and in this way sustain a mentoring relationship throughout its progressing phases. It often depends on the maturity and personality of the mentee as to which is the best style to use.

---

88   Ibid., 36.

MAINTAIN YOUR RELATIONSHIP WITH GOD

The ministry mentor needs to continue growing as a person and servant of the Lord to be effective. As mentioned, a mentor is not someone who has already become perfect but is one who is moving toward excellence. This movement is especially important in the area of maintaining a relationship with God. The apostle Paul was transparent about his spiritual journey. He invited his mentees to observe and imitate him (Philippians 3:12–17). The best gift of a mentor to a mentee is a godly life that flows from an ever-deepening relationship with God.

The mentor is always conscious that the mentee is observing his or her life. For instance, the disciples of Jesus watched him when he prayed and wanted to learn from him how to pray. It became a teaching opportunity. The spiritual habits and practices of the mentor, as observed by mentees, become opportunities to teach them. Ministry mentors need to be aware that those being mentored by them are watching not only their ministry skills but also their lifestyle and attitudes. Mentees in ministry will ask questions of their mentors relating to their whole life.

SELF-AWARENESS AND EMOTIONAL INTELLIGENCE

Mentors need to be self-aware and understand the impact their words and actions have on their mentees. Self-awareness involves being emotionally intelligent, which is having the ability to recognize your emotions and understanding what they're telling you. It includes knowing how your emotions affect people around you, and having the capacity to perceive the emotions of others and understand how they feel. Further, emotional intelligence includes the ability to manage relationships effectively. In Chapter Eight, we will discuss matters related to the mentee's self-awareness. Prospective mentors will find it helpful for themselves to apply the same principles and questions to discover where they are at in their own life and ministry journeys.

SELF-CARE

Be an example to your mentee by maintaining the right balance between your ministry and personal life. They are likely to emulate what they see in you. Build into your life that which keeps you physically, emotionally, and spiritually healthy. Monitor all the relationships in your life. If you have children, spend enough time with them to be a good parent; if you are married, be a good spouse; if your parents are still alive, honour them. Be an example to your mentees as well. Let them get a glimpse of how you live, even in contexts outside of formal ministry.

Some pastors are so tied up in their ministry that if you take that away, they have nothing. That isn't healthy. Sometimes they cannot say no, so they take on more responsibility than they can realistically handle. They wear themselves out and fail to pay attention to the other areas of their lives. If a mentor doesn't take care of all matters in his or her own life and ministry, it will be difficult to guide another effectively.

When we have a broad foundation in our lives, our ministries will be much stronger. The mentee needs to observe how we operate out of a large and balanced foundation.

PRODUCTIVE AND COMPETENT

The best ministry mentors keep active in ministry, always being ready to take on new challenges. They continue to grow and never stop learning. They model this attitude to their mentees. For the mentee who is serious about improving, it is a great encouragement and inspiration to see their mentor continually pushing forward. It is an opportunity for both the mentor and mentee to share in the journey of growth.

The mentor also needs to be competent. First, she needs to be competent in the ministry context in which she serves and to strive continuously for excellence. It is good for the mentee to be able to have confidence in her ability. But she also needs to be competent in the application of mentoring skills. The mentor needs to understand how to transfer her wisdom and knowledge to the mentee in a beneficial way.

As a mentor, you need to assess your current life and ministry situation to make sure that you will be able to serve your mentee where you are in your life and ministry journey. For instance, if you are dealing with major issues which may have the potential for an adverse impact, you should not be mentoring anyone unless they are mature enough to process with you what is taking place.

HOLD YOURSELF ACCOUNTABLE

For you as a mentor to remain credible, it is essential to be honest, consistent, and have integrity in your relationships. Honour commitments to yourself, your mentee, and others in your life and ministry. It is better to under-promise and over-deliver than to over-promise and under-deliver. If you have a failure in this area, admit to it and deal with it. Do not cover up. It is also good to build accountability relationships into your life, people to whom you answer. They can be mentors, coaches, friends, prayer partners, fellow team members, co-workers, or spiritual directors. Small groups such as those found within a cell church structure can also help to hold you accountable. People in the group are usually able to discern how you are doing from week to week.

Being accountable to someone else regarding your mentoring relationship is important. You do not need to share details, but let some person (possibly your own mentor) be aware of how your mentoring activity and relationships are proceeding.

HUMILITY

As a Christian ministry mentor, one of your most important virtues should be humility. John Dickson, who explores this subject in his book *Humilitas*, provides a definition:

Humility is the noble choice to forego your status, deploy your resources or use your influence for the good of others before yourself.[89]

Jesus modelled this when he stooped down to wash his disciples' feet. It is interesting to observe that authentic humility is connected to self-awareness:

> *Jesus knew that the Father had put all things under his power, and that he had come from God and was returning to God; so he got up from the meal, took off his outer clothing, and wrapped a towel around his waist.*
> —John 13:3–4

We can also observe humility in the gracious acceptance of limitations as well as in transparency with respect to weaknesses and faults. As we admit our shortcomings and mistakes, the mentee is then free to be human as well. We should apologize when appropriate and not be afraid to say "I don't know."

However, humility does not mean we have to function from a posture of perpetual self-doubt. A humble attitude speaks of sober self-assessment. The apostle Paul expresses it like this: *"Do not think of yourself more highly than you ought, but rather think of yourself with sober judgment, in accordance with the faith God has distributed to each of you"* (Romans 12:3). As a mentor, model confident humility.

BURDEN OF POWER AND IDEALIZATION

Whether we like it or not, there is power in a mentoring relationship. The degree of power often depends on the personal influence you have in other contexts. The mentoring relationship may itself lead to some power because of the respect the mentor gains from the mentee. It may also be because in some cases there is a supervisory component to the relationship.

---

89 John P. Dickson, *Humilitas: A Lost Key to Life, Love, and Leadership*, Kindle edition (Grand Rapids, MI: Zondervan, 2011), location 167.

Whatever power the mentor may have in the relationship, it is never appropriate to abuse it. Power in this relationship should be used only for the benefit of the mentee. The mentor may use power to encourage and support, but never to exploit or take unfair advantage of the mentee.

At the beginning of the relationship, it is also possible that the mentor may be looked on with a high level of respect. He may have a kind of hero status. It may be uncomfortable for the mentor to be placed at that level by the mentee, because he understands that it may create unrealistic expectations. The mentor should deal with this graciously. It can be a good thing, since it does strengthen the relationship in the early phases.

Figure 3: Mentoring Relationship Maturation Progression

But the relationship should mature wherein the mentee continues to identify with the mentor but also gains a more realistic perception of who the mentor is. Idealization needs to shift toward healthy identification. As this happens, the mentee takes on some of the desired traits of the mentor. The mentee sees the mentor in a more realistic light and often imitates the mentor, taking on some of his style of ministry. While this is an expected outcome, the mentor needs to encourage the mentee to develop his or her own style. God has given everyone their own gifts, abilities, and personalities which need to emerge. In other words, the mentor should not try to make the mentee into a copy of him or herself. Ultimately, mentees mature in their own ministry as unique individuals who make their own contribution. Here the mentee has completed the process of individuation. Johnson and Ridley state, "If tolerated well, idealization will allow your protégé to move from clone to colleague. That is the goal."[90]

Throughout the various phases of the relationship, the mentor should point to Christ as the ultimate mentor and say, as Paul did, *"Follow*

---

90 Johnson and Ridley, 60.

my example, as I follow the example of Christ" (1 Corinthians 11:1). For the Christian ministry mentee, Christ remains the ideal and the one we all must follow.

INTENTIONAL AND TRANSPARENT MODELLING

Being a mentor is more than just having discussions and dispensing advice. It is also about demonstrating life and service in an intentional way so that mentees can observe their mentors in real-life situations. Many nuances and subtleties cannot be discussed or taught; they need to be seen in action. Also, things observed are much more easily remembered. So whenever it is possible and practical, mentors should create situations where mentees can watch them in action. This is how Jesus mentored his disciples. This was also a part of the apostle Paul's method. He was intentional and transparent.

> *We did this… in order to offer ourselves as a model for you to imitate.*
> —2 Thessalonians 3:9

He invited people to follow his example. The credibility of mentorship often rests on mentees having seen their mentor in action. If direct observation isn't possible or practical, mentees can indirectly observe as the mentor shares what they have done, said, and thought in various situations.

Both character traits and ministry skills should be modelled. Being an example, or modelling behaviour, is often done unconsciously. It is better when it's unconscious because it can then be genuine and real. But the mentor does need to be aware that he or she is being observed by the mentee. This can be a real incentive to stay sharp in all areas for the purpose of an excellent mentoring relationship. Mentees should see how mentors bring to bear their character traits in the different roles they play. The mentor may play different roles, but the character should be consistent. In other words, the mentor may wear different hats but always have the same face.

Be Relational and Wise

As we have defined it, mentoring is a relationship built on mutual trust, so the mentor must, of course, be relational. Some find it easier than others, but wherever you find yourself on the introvert-extrovert scale, connect with your mentee on a personal level. This will involve at least some degree of vulnerability, but as you engage the mentee relationally, you will need to be wise. Not every mentee will be comfortable with open exchanges of a personal nature. Nor can we assume that every mentee will be trustworthy with respect to the information that is shared. There is also the possibility that they may misunderstand what the relationship means.

How Transparent Should a Mentor Be?

While it is good for the mentor to be transparent for the benefit of the mentee, some aspects of self-disclosure should be measured in relation to the level of trust between them (see Figure 4). It is not always appropriate for the mentor to allow the mentee to know everything about them, but the mentor should self-disclose when it may be helpful for the learning of the mentee.

A certain level of self-disclosure about the struggles the mentor has faced can encourage the mentee as they face similar struggles. Appropriate self-disclosure puts the seemingly unreachable achievements of the mentor into proper perspective. This also reduces the temptation for the mentor to appear as a perfect hero to the mentee. The mentor should not allow herself to be seen at such a high place that the mentee can never reach her.

A mentor may be a little like a hero at the beginning of the relationship, but judicious self-disclosure will humanize them. The mentor should not try to appear as someone who has mastered every challenge but as someone who by the grace of God has experienced successes and endured disappointments. The mentee is likely to learn much from how the mentor has worked through his or her weaknesses, but the primary motive in sharing such experiences should be to help the mentee grow in their own life and ministry.

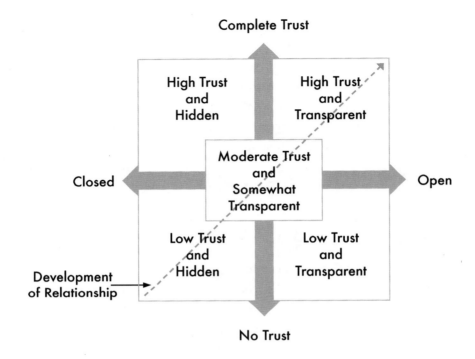

Figure 4: Gauging Appropriate Self-Disclosure in a Mentoring Relationship

Accept Increasing Friendship and Mutuality

Mentoring relationships develop as trust levels rise and openness increases. The dynamics also change, similar to the way a parent's relationship develops from relating to a younger child, to a teenage child, and to an adult child according to the level of their maturity. In a ministry mentoring context, mutuality develops as the mentor and mentee share a greater repertoire of experiences. They increasingly relate to one another on a similar level, and friendship develops. This kind of development is to be expected.

We see an analogous progression in the relationship between Jesus and his disciples. Jesus was able to say to them, *"I no longer call you servants, because a servant does not know his master's business. Instead, I have called you friends, for everything that I learned from my Father I have made known to you"* (John

15:15). Friendships which begin as a result of formal mentoring often continue long after the initial arrangement is concluded.

In some mentoring relationships, a development of friendship may be difficult because of the mentee's view of hierarchical relationships. A mentee in such a case may not feel comfortable with a more collegial relationship with the mentor because of the perceived power distance between them. The mentor will need to be sensitive and pay attention to the comfort level of the mentee. Not all mentoring relationships will develop into friendships, but they can still fulfill the mentee's learning objectives.

ENCOURAGE WITHOUT BECOMING BLIND

When the relationship between the mentor and mentee becomes stronger, a potential danger could be that the mentor becomes blind to the faults of the mentee. It is important for the mentor to be honest in their ongoing evaluation of the mentee and confront with frankness the issues that arise. As you encourage the advance of the mentee, keep an eye out for dysfunctions that need to be addressed. Failure to do so at the earlier stages of leadership development will set your mentee up for a fall later.

DO NOT EXPECT PERFECTION

Do not expect perfection in yourself or your mentee. Perfectionism leads to negativity and unrealistic evaluations. It also creates performance anxiety, adding unnecessary stress to those who fall under its spell. A more appropriate and helpful approach to life and ministry begins with the understanding that the God who designed us for a purpose is at work in us (Philippians 1:6 and Ephesians 2:10). We are a work in progress and therefore we've not yet arrived where we might like to be. This was modelled by the apostle Paul, who continued to strive toward the purpose Christ had for him while acknowledging that he was not perfect (Philippians 3:12

– 14). As mentioned earlier in this chapter, we can hold a value of excellence without insisting on perfection.

RESPECT PRIVACY AND PROTECT CONFIDENTIALITY

The mentee needs to feel safe with the mentor to maximize the benefit of the mentoring relationship. This includes having confidence that what is shared privately will not be made public or be shared with someone else. If the mentoring relationship, however, is of a supervisory nature, it will be necessary for the mentor and mentee to be clear as to what can remain confidential. If the mentor is also the mentee's supervisor, a discussion between them will help set the boundaries in this area.

It is also important that the mentor does not unduly pry into the private matters of the mentee, forcing them to share things that have no bearing on the ministry mentoring agenda.

USE HUMOUR

The appropriate use of humour can help to reduce anxiety in mentees who may have just begun their ministry journey. Mentors can help the mentees learn not to take themselves too seriously by injecting humour into the relationship. A mentor may occasionally share a funny incident that happened to him in a ministry context. Or he may help the mentee see something they experience together from a lighter side. A healthy mix of work and laughter can go a long way to strengthen the mentoring relationship, and ministry effectiveness in general. However, never use humour to belittle a mentee or to put anyone in their ministry context in a bad light.

GET RID OF JEALOUSY

Sometimes the gifts, qualities, and skills of a mentee exceed that of the mentor in some areas, and the mentor may feel tempted to become jealous. Jealousy undermines mentoring and signals that the mentor needs to deal with their fears and insecurities. A biblical example is that of Saul becoming jealous of David. Saul invited him to the king's table as part of a mentoring imitative, but when the people perceived David as being more successful than Saul, Saul began to sabotage and undermine David.

From the outset of the relationship, the mentor's goal should be to see the mentee grow—and if possible, exceed—the mentor. Celebrate the success of the mentee, but also help them to evaluate their success with grace and humility. That is, after all, what the mentoring relationship is all about.

If jealousy becomes an insurmountable problem for the mentor, it may be best to hand the mentee over to another mentor while the first mentor works on her fears and insecurities. Her self-awareness as a mentor is paramount.

THE HEART OF A MENTOR IS GENEROUS

Good mentors do not think of themselves first. They will always have an eye open to see what their mentees need in their journey toward effective ministry and be ready to invest in the mentees as much as they can. They consider what is best for the mentee and the kingdom of God. They ask the question, "How can I help this mentee with his or her unique gifts, abilities, and skills to advance the kingdom of God?" That is the guiding question of a ministry mentoring relationship in all its phases.

In these two chapters, we have looked at what the mentor does and who the mentor is. In the next chapter, we will see how a mentor can discover who the mentee is, and what they will need from the mentor.

QUESTIONS: FROM REFLECTION TO ACTION

1. In addition to what is mentioned in this chapter, what are some values you hold that make you a good mentor?
2. What is your preferred mentoring style? Are you people-oriented or task-oriented? Or somewhere in between? Why do you think so?
3. What habits of yours would you like to impart to a mentee because you know the value of those habits to your own life and ministry?
4. Have you seen anything in this chapter you would have to address before you begin a mentoring relationship? What will you do and how will you do it?

Chapter Eight

WHO THE MENTEE IS—MENTORING AWARENESS

THE MOVIE *THE KARATE KID* TELLS A STORY ABOUT THE MENTORING RELATIONSHIP between Mr. Miyagi, an older man, and Daniel, a teenage boy.[91]

Through a series of events, Daniel discovers that Mr. Miyagi is a karate master. Daniel is being bullied and urgently needs to learn how to defend himself, so he asks Mr. Miyagi to teach him karate. Mr. Miyagi recognizes that Daniel's motives are not entirely in keeping with the underlying philosophy of karate that Mr. Miyagi holds to, but the older man understands Daniel's desperate need. They negotiate, and Mr. Miyagi agrees to teach Daniel karate with the condition that Daniel will not question his training methods. There is enough trust in their relationship for Daniel to accept those terms, even though that trust is tested at times.

Daniel's learning objective is to learn karate, but Mr. Miyagi understands through experience that Daniel must also learn other things for this objective to be satisfactorily achieved. So he maps out critical growth pathways that promise to get Daniel where he wants to go. In the process, he also helps Daniel learn life lessons that he not may have been aware he needed.

The story illustrates how a mentee's awareness of their own shortcomings can lead into the mentoring agenda. The mentee's awareness of this knowledge gap comes as the result of a crisis moment. The mentor, as a guide, can help the mentee find the help he needs. At the same time, he points to other potential growth areas in the mentee's life that need to be nurtured. If we apply this process to a ministry mentee, growing in those

---

91 *The Karate Kid*, directed by John G. Avildsen (Los Angeles, CA: Columbia Pictures Corporation, 1984).

areas will sustain them through their life and ministry, allowing them to gain new skills that will increase their competency.

Note that in a ministry mentoring relationship, we are usually dealing with adult learners and don't need to be as mysterious as Mr. Miyagi about our critical growth pathways, but experienced mentors do see things that their mentees may not yet see. Jesus, too, led his disciples along critical growth pathways which they did not always understand, even though they had specific things they wanted to learn from their mentor (John 15:15 and 16:12).

TOWARD A MENTORING AGENDA

People come to the ministry in different ways. They also have various ministry assignments. The implication for this is that every aspiring minister will have unique learning needs.

For instance, let us compare the stories of Ralph and Susan. Ralph grew up in a Christian home and attended church throughout his life. At a youth camp, he received Jesus Christ as his Saviour and experienced a profound change within his life from that time on. When Ralph graduated from high school, he heard the call to ministry and went to Bible college for training. After Ralph concluded theological education, he was invited to be the pastor of a small struggling church in a suburb of the city. Despite his experience and training, Ralph still found that he didn't know how to transition this congregation into a healthy growing church, so he approached an older pastor in his denomination and asked for guidance. The pastor agreed to mentor and guide him in acquiring the leadership skills required for his ministry assignment. This was the mentoring agenda.

Susan, on the other hand, came to Christian faith when she was thirty years old. Until she met a Christian who told her about Christ at her office job, she had little knowledge of faith. Her family followed another faith but was not very serious about it. Because Susan had developed a medical condition that made it difficult to work, her Christian friend invited her to a small group meeting of Christians who prayed for her healing. In a very short time, her condition improved and she received Christ. She volunteered to serve in the church, but over time the leaders recognized that she had the dedication, gifting, and calling for full-time ministry engagement. Susan was a gifted administrator, but she did not feel confident in dealing with many of the spiritual issues of the people she encountered in her role. She felt that she lacked pastoral skills. When Susan mentioned her concerns to her senior pastor, he referred her to someone who could mentor and guide her on the critical growth pathways that would strengthen her pastoral skills.

There are, of course, many possible scenarios, and each represents different knowledge gaps that need to be closed to increase the individual's capacity for ministry. This is about more than adding information to a mentee's knowledge base, however; it may also be about developing resources that are already within a mentee. These need to be released. The mentor facilitates the access of both the external and internal storehouses of knowledge.

We have seen how the felt need of a mentee leads to the mentoring agenda, and how that determines the learning objectives of the mentoring relationship. From the mentoring agenda, the critical growth pathways are mapped out for the next phases of the mentee's learning journey. The question asked at this point is "What are the steps the mentee needs to take to get to the next level?" These are determined through negotiations between the mentor and the mentee. We will discuss this further in Chapter Ten.

The mentoring agenda will ultimately derive from a negotiation between two perspectives. The mentor and mentee bring their perspectives to the table:

- What the mentor believes is good for the mentee.
- What the mentee wants to learn.

If the mentoring relationship has been initiated in the interests, or through the agency, of a church or ministry organization, certain ministry objectives may also need to be considered as the agenda is set. Somehow at the end of the negotiation, all parties must feel satisfied that the established agenda and development plan promises to fulfill the purpose of the mentoring relationship and help the mentee grow as a person, minister, and leader.

But there are other matters to consider, matters which will assist the mentor to guide the setting of the agenda so that it can have deeper and wider impact.

KNOWING THE STORY OF THE MENTEE'S LIFE

An important part of establishing the mentoring agenda is for the mentor to know the story of the mentee. Reese and Loane suggest that "if we are going to walk alongside others, seeking to pay attention with them to what God is up to in their lives, then we must pay attention to the story of their lives."[92]

Questions need to be asked about the life and ministry journey that brought the mentee to seek mentorship. What are the factors that shaped them in the past, and what continues to shape them in the present? Are there defining moments, experiences, people, and circumstances that need to be highlighted as indicators of God's guiding presence in their lives? These can be marked on a timeline to help identify the patterns and recurring themes in the mentee's life which explain their current reality. These can also indicate where their life and ministry journey is taking them.

This "big picture" view of the mentee's journey brings clarity, helping the mentor locate where the mentee is in his or her leadership journey. At the same time, it helps keep their long-term objectives and purposes in view.[93]

A timeline approach pays attention to what God has been doing in the past and how life experiences have impacted the mentee. As these are narrated, the mentor needs to hear the story as it is told, listening for significant events in the mentee's life and the ways in which the mentee responded to those experiences. At some point in the mentoring relationship, the mentor may offer different perspectives to help the mentee process those life events in the most beneficial way.

---

92   Reese and Loane, 57.

93   Both J. Robert Clinton's *The Making of a Leader* and Randy D. Reese and Robert Loane's *Deep Mentoring* provide a detailed explanation of such an approach.

Figure 5: Mentoring Agenda Overview: The Timeline Approach

Here we have discussed the mentee's story in terms of *what was*. Next, we will turn to consider the importance of understanding the current reality, in terms of *what is*. Then, in Chapter Nine, we will see how the critical growth pathways can be crafted, leading toward *what will be*—where the mentee wants to go.

NUDGING THE MENTEE TOWARD SELF-AWARENESS

Carson Pue, in his book *Mentoring Leaders: Wisdom for Developing Character, Calling, and Competency*, illustrates the importance of self-awareness with a sailing metaphor. He and his wife were learning how to sail. He describes a teaching moment when their instructor asked them, "What is the most important thing to know regarding navigation?" After several unsuccessful attempts at answering that question, they listened carefully as the instructor finally revealed the truth: "The most significant thing in navigation—the very most important piece of information—is knowing exactly where you are."[94]

To successfully and safely navigate the journey of life and ministry, the mentee needs to take the time to understand who they are as a person and where they are at this point in their development journey. This knowledge is called self-awareness.

---

94 Carson Pue, *Mentoring Leaders: Wisdom for Developing Character, Calling, and Competency* (Grand Rapids, MI: Baker Books, 2005), 31.

Locating the Mentee on the Spiritual Journey

Self-awareness for the mentee involves understanding their strengths, weaknesses, gifts, and passions. This includes being aware of how their life intersects with others. But most importantly, it is about their relationship with God. The primary and core question is this: "Where are you in your relationship to Jesus?"[95] As they probe deeper, mentees can be encouraged to ask themselves, "Who am I in Christ and how do I express that in my life and ministry?"

These are basic discipleship questions from which we will never graduate. In working with emerging Christian leaders in the role of mentors, we cannot assume that these questions are adequately dealt with in the lives of our mentees. We must take the time to pause there and encourage deep reflection. In fact, they should be invited to ask these questions regularly, as a matter of habit. This is an important part in the spiritual formation of those who aspire to serve in ministry.

It is also worthwhile for the mentee to understand the temptations to which they are exposed. A standard short list of these is money, sex, and power. But there are other temptations, such as pride, laziness, selfishness, and lack of self-control. Scripture identifies many temptations which work against a godly life. If these are not overcome, they have the potential to short-circuit ministry.[96] Each of these is a potential talking point that the mentor can raise with the mentee on the leadership development journey.

There may also be areas in the mentee's life from which they need to be delivered. This may involve debilitating past experiences, unhealthy relationships, and deeply rooted addictions which both the mentee and mentor cannot ignore. These may or may not have been uncovered as the mentor gets to know the mentee's story. Steps need to be taken so that the mentee will be freed up to grow into what God has intended for him or her.[97] Failing to deal with these areas in a decisive manner will stunt the mentee's spiritual growth.

---

95 Ibid., 40.
96 See, for instance, Galatians 5:19–21; Ephesians 4:17–32; Colossians 3:5–9; James 3:14; and Matthew 15:18–20.
97 For a fuller discussion, see Pue, 57–75.

A part of becoming self-aware in this core identity is to do an assessment of where the mentee is in his or her spiritual journey. One way to do this is by using the model of Christian Formation in Figure 6.

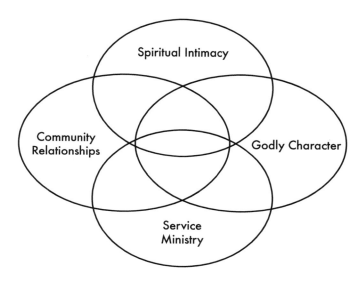

Figure 6: A Model of Christian Formation[98]

- Spiritual Intimacy: What is the quality of their relationship with God?
    - What does their devotional life look like?
    - How would they describe their regular time alone with God?
    - How is their prayer life?
    - How is their engagement with Scripture?
    - How do they express worship?
    - How would they describe their knowledge of God?
    - How do they express their love for God?

---

98 The graphic is adapted from Stephen A. Brown, *Leading Me: Eight Practices for a Christian Leader's Most Important Assignment* (Lagoon City, Brechin, ON: Castle Quay Books, 2015), 41.

- Community Relationships: What is the quality of their relationships with the people in their life?
  - How do they relate to other Christians? In their church? Small group? In other churches?
  - What is their family life like? How do they relate to their family members? Spouses? Children? Parents? Siblings? In-laws?
  - How do they relate to people in general?
  - How do they express God's grace and generosity to others?
  - Are they forgiving?
- Godly Character: How Christ-like are they?
  - What aspects of the fruit of the Spirit are present?
  - How do their ethics reflect biblical instructions?
  - How do they manage their emotions?
  - Are they able to control their physical desires in appropriate ways?
  - Do they show evidence of humility combined with confidence?
- Service: What attitudes do they have as they serve in ministry?
  - How do they serve God?
  - How do they serve fellow Christians?
  - How do they serve those outside the Christian faith?
  - Do they use their gifts to serve others?
  - Do they understand their sphere of ministry?
  - Are they prepared to support others?
  - How well do they work on a ministry team?
  - Is their ministry attitude characterized by a "kingdom of God" mentality?
  - Do they acknowledge with gratitude what God is doing through other ministry initiatives?

This checklist of questions is suggestive of the kinds of things a mentor can ask her mentee to pinpoint where he is in his spiritual journey. The answers will assist the mentor in knowing the mentee's spiritual maturity.

Not all the questions need to be asked of the mentee directly, since many of the answers can be acquired by observation. Nor is it prudent to rush these questions. The mentor needs to encourage the mentee to take the time to process these questions. The mentee should consider scheduling a personal spiritual retreat for a few days to work through the issues these questions might bring to the surface.

The mentor needs to be particularly sensitive to what the Holy Spirit is doing in the mentee's life. The purpose of an assessment like this is to help both the mentor and mentee identify the critical issues which need to be brought into the mentoring agenda.

Understanding the Giftedness Set of the Mentee

Self-awareness also relates to what can be called the giftedness set, referring to a combination of natural abilities, acquired skills, and spiritual gifting.[99]

Natural abilities are those capacities with which we were born, such as intelligence, physical attributes, and some aspects of personality. These are the traits we have inherited from our biological parents—our DNA.

Acquired skills come to us through our upbringing and from the environments to which we have needed to adapt. They are enhanced through education, job experience, the influence of significant people in our lives, and generally the experiences we have over time.

Spiritual gifts are abilities that come to us by the enablement of the Holy Spirit.[100] They are supernatural in that they surpass what can be accomplished through natural abilities and acquired skills. Sometimes these gifts are obviously supernatural manifestations that accompany those who serve in ministry, such as healing and miracles. Other times spiritual gifts just enhance a natural ability or acquired skill for greater impact. For instance, consider a person who has a natural ability to teach. Through training and

---

99   This concept is helpfully described in Robert and Richard Clinton's *Unlocking Your Giftedness* (40).
100 Romans 12:4–8; 1 Corinthians 12, 14; and Ephesians 4:1.

experience, she adds teaching skills. She may then also receive the spiritual gift of teaching by which she can supernaturally express spiritual truth with extraordinary clarity. As people listen, their eyes are opened to spiritual truth in ways that cannot be explained naturally.

While it is useful to be aware of the components of the mentee's giftedness set, I do not believe it is always necessary to distinguish these elements. In a sense, they all come from God and are part of the total design of the individual.

Earlier in this chapter, we spoke of paying attention to what God was doing in the life of the mentee. When the mentor knows the mentee's story, their giftedness set will often emerge out of the story. Of course, part of the role of the mentor is to narrate the story back to mentees in ways that they become more self-aware of their giftedness set. The mentor encourages the mentee to build on that and grow in the use of natural abilities, continue to acquire more skills, and *"eagerly desire gifts of the Spirit"* (1 Corinthians 14:1).

It is not within the purview of this book to examine the various components of the giftedness set in detail, but it is nonetheless helpful to use that framework to lead the mentee to understand what his capacities currently are and what can be realistically done to develop them.

In addition to what is presented in this book, mentors will need to design their own questions, raising issues relevant to the mentee's ministry and cultural context. There are also tools available on various ministry websites which can be used to facilitate one's self-awareness of the areas we have addressed.[101] Whichever instruments and questions are used, the purpose is to nudge the mentee toward self-awareness.

---

101 For instance, note the S.H.A.P.E. assessment tool, as found in Erik Rees's *S.H.A.P.E.: Finding & Fulfilling Your Unique Purpose for Life* (Grand Rapids, MI: Zondervan, 2006). For the online version, see www.shapediscovery.com. See also Peter Scazzero, *Emotionally Healthy Spirituality: Unleash a Revolution in Your Life in Christ* (Nashville, TN: Integrity, 2006). For the Emotionally Healthy Spirituality assessment tool, see www.emotionallyhealthy.org/personalassessment. A simple DISC personality test is available at www.123test.com/disc-personality-test. Waiver note: I provide these links only for convenience. They were available at the time of writing. I do not have any connection with the providers of the assessment resources mentioned nor do I guarantee the accuracy of those assessments.

Having understood the importance of understanding the past journey and the current reality of the mentee, we will discuss in the next chapter the ongoing development journey.

QUESTIONS: FROM REFLECTION TO ACTION

1. Before considering the story of the mentee, how important is it for you as a mentor to understand your own story?
2. What are some of your favourite ways to start a discussion to help someone tell you their story?
3. Why do all the dimensions of Christian Formation need to be considered for a person in ministry?
4. What are some of the ways in which you can determine the giftedness set of your mentee?

Chapter Nine

HOW THE MENTEE LEARNS—THE MENTORING AGENDA

WE WERE IN A GOVERNMENT OFFICE WITH OUR TEENAGE CHILDREN, PAINSTAKINGLY filling out visa application forms. We showed them how to do it and submitted the forms together. Then we anxiously waited for our visas to be granted so we could get on with our journey to the next country on our itinerary. Usually I was the one dealing with visa matters on behalf of the family, but in this case we all had to be present.

The long wait tested our collective patience. The weather was hot and muggy and the waiting area wasn't a comfortable place.

"Why is it taking so long?" the children complained. "We've been here for hours!"

Since I wasn't new to this kind of waiting game, I answered with my tongue firmly in cheek: "This is designed to be a character-building experience."

They rolled their eyes at this dadism, but the point was made. I know they got it because the character-building phrase became an inside family joke that was used whenever any of us started to get irritated at life.

So they learned not only the important travel skill of filling out forms, but also how to be patient. The whole experience became a mentoring opportunity, developing both character and competency.

DEVELOPMENT OF CHARACTER AND COMPETENCY

For the sake of simplicity, we'll look at the mentee's capacity as a minister in terms of these two development categories: character and competency.

You will note the correspondence between these and what we have discussed in Chapter Eight. Spiritual maturity relates to character, and the giftedness set to competency.

Character development includes such things as growth in spirituality, increase in emotional maturity, and progress in relational abilities. Competency development may include such elements as deepening intellectual ability, widening communication skills, and strengthening various other ministry gifts and skills. Any of the areas in these two categories become an inherent part of the mentoring agenda or learning objectives.

In ministry contexts, the character and competency of an individual complement each other. Ministry credibility hangs on both. Therefore, the ministry mentoring agenda must have a dual track approach. There must be custom-designed critical growth pathways for the continued development of Christian character based on the level of the mentee's spiritual maturity. At the same time, uniquely planned critical growth pathways must be in place to help strengthen the mentee's ministry skills based on their needs. These critical growth pathways need to be negotiated at the early stages of the mentoring relationship.

The Priority of Character Development

For Christian ministry mentoring, paying attention to the character development of the mentee is paramount because the primary identity of the Christian minister doesn't reside in the ministry role or position but on who they are as a Christian. Therefore, whatever ministry skills the mentee wishes to strengthen, the priority must be on growing as a devoted follower of Christ.

In relation to this priority, various spiritual disciplines can be incorporated into a development plan in order to form, strengthen, and sustain Christ-like character. I speak of nothing other than being a disciplined follower of Jesus Christ by pursuing the pathway of discipleship to which he has called us all. But the urgency for such discipleship increases as one advances further on a ministry journey that involves serving in Christian leadership.

The Plan for Competency Development

It is here that critical growth pathways may diverge for different mentees, since each one will come into a mentoring relationship with specific learning needs. As mentioned previously, the mentoring agenda needs to be negotiated by the mentor and mentee. The ministry organization, as a stakeholder in the mentoring relationship, may also have some requirements about what the mentee needs to learn.

As we discuss the critical pathways for competency development, we will consider different aspects of the learning that may need to occur. The basic ministry skillset needs to be acquired, certainly, but then there's also the contextual application of those skills. Finally, there's the strategic implementation aspect.

The analogy of learning how to ride a bicycle will help us to understand these three elements. To learn how to ride a bike, we need to learn various skills which must be used in perfect coordination. The rider needs to know how to push the pedals so that he can move forward. At the same time, he needs to use the handlebar correctly to steer. As he pedals and steers, he must also keep himself in balance. To complete the basic skillset for riding a bike, he must also know how to apply the brakes and stop the bike without falling.

For these skills to be useful, he also needs to know how to ride his bike in different settings. Sometimes he may ride his bike in a tranquil rural area, and other times he may ride along the busy streets of a city. He needs to understand how to ride his bike in harmony with other riders, and even other vehicles and pedestrians that share the road. Each context will determine how basic bike-riding skills need to be applied.

But the ability to ride a bicycle in different contexts is only helpful when the rider can discern when it is appropriate to use that mode of transportation. Perhaps someone else should take the trip. Are there better ways to ride the bike? Are there alterations that could be made to improve the bike to make it more efficient?

We could go on and develop the analogy, but I think we have made the point that there are different levels of knowledge and skills. The mentee may have already learned the basic skills in a school context, or by simple observation, and may not always need a mentor to help them appropriate those skills. But at the higher levels, a mentor is an indispensable guide to help the mentee navigate the subtle nuances of ministry context and the complexities of ministry systems. A spiritually mature mentor will also be able to discern the movements of the Holy Spirit in the life of the mentee, as well as the ministry context.

Basic skills. The core competencies in ministry could include the ability to do many things, such as preaching, praying, teaching, administration, governance, counselling, writing, conflict management, evangelism, church planting, visitation, praying for the sick, baptizing, administering the Lord's supper, conducting funerals, making disciples, developing lay leaders, time management, social services, fundraising, leadership, vision casting, mobilizing, developing ministry strategies, shepherding, prophesying, and facilitating small groups, among others.

I am sure you can think of many other ministry activities you could add to the list. These require skills, some of which can be learned in school, from written materials, by observation, and by experience. A mentor can facilitate the learning of many of these by helping the mentee fill in the missing pieces of knowledge and understanding. He can teach directly or refer the mentee to other resources such as books, articles, and courses. The mentor can hold the mentee accountable to the learning objectives.

Contextual application. But most often a mentor helps a mentee with the contextual application of ministry skills. She does this by creating awareness of the ministry context and by teaching the mentee how her unique blend of ministry giftedness can be most effective in achieving the mentee's ministry objectives.

For instance, when Elizabeth and I went to Tanzania to serve as missionaries, we already had some experience in ministry. We had acquired some of the basic ministry skills we needed for the assignment. But we had to learn how to apply these in a new context. One seasoned missionary gave us the best possible advice for the time: "When you come into that new environment, suspend judgment on what you see and hear. Keep quiet, watch, listen, and learn for one year before offering your opinion on anything."

As new missionaries, we did our best to follow that advice. We had to learn a new language, understand a new culture, and adapt to a new ministry context. We had the help of other missionaries who became mentors for us, but also the help of local ministers who were willing to introduce us to the realities of ministry from an insider perspective. They taught us about certain things foreigners sometimes do which might be inappropriate and therefore misunderstood by those we were serving. They instructed us in the way things were done in that context. As we grew in our understanding of the nuances of ministry, we could adapt our ministry skills accordingly.

Strategic implementation. Strategic implementation of ministry skills can be described as using the right ministry skills in the right place at the right time for the right reasons in harmony with others and for purposes that advance the kingdom of God. This first involves asking the big questions of calling, vision, mission, and purpose. Secondly, it means bringing one's personal vision into alignment with the corporate vision—for instance, the vision of a team, an organization, or a church. Then goals are set, plans are made, action is taken, evaluation is done, and the cycle is repeated as required. These steps are most often taken in concert with other people on a ministry team, but in some ministry assignments they are done alone. In such cases especially, the mentor can play a significant role.

Strategic implementation means understanding what is taking place from different perspectives. For instance, a mentor who is outside the ministry authority structure of the mentee may be in a good position to provide a broader perspective on how the mentee's giftedness set can be leveraged for maximum impact. There are also times when a minister senses that it's time to move out of a particular ministry context and into another context, or he is invited to take on a different ministry role. The mentor can help the mentee process these kinds of transitions, strategically considering the big picture of what God has been doing in the mentee's life.

DETERMINE THE MENTORING AGENDA

Everything we have said in the last chapter, and so far in this chapter, has helped us to establish the learning needs. We have considered the big picture of the mentee's life: *what was, what is,* and *what will be.* This all provides the background for the mentoring agenda.

The discussion must then move on to focus on *what is next.* If the mentoring partners do not move purposefully into next steps, the mentorship will lose momentum.

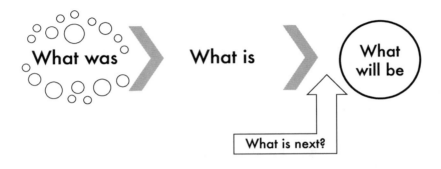

Figure 7: The Mentoring Agenda Focus

You may already have a list of possible learning objectives by now. If not, it will be useful to create such a list as you engage the mentee. Some of the items on the list will come from the felt learning needs of the mentee and will usually be expressed directly by the mentee. Others you will be able to identify as you get to know the mentee. Still others may be suggested by various people in the organization who have a stake in the mentoring relationship.

I suggest that you categorize the potential learning objectives under the headings "Character" and "Competency." This is primarily for your reference as you negotiate the mentoring agenda. It may not be possible to include all the items in a mentoring agenda, but having them recorded in some way may enable you to address those issues indirectly as the mentoring relationship progresses. But the central question relates to the priorities: "What should be the learning focus of the mentoring relationship now?" As the mentor, you need to remember that the mentee drives the relationship, and you as mentor are the guide. Consider these things as you set the mentoring agenda together:

- What is the mentee currently motivated to work on?
- What are the new skills required for a particular ministry task that the mentee is currently involved in?
- What skills will be needed later and take more time to develop?
- What spiritual and character matters need to be addressed now?

Based on these questions, you can set the mentoring agenda. The Mentoring Agenda Process Worksheet in Appendix A can assist you in this.

SET THE LEARNING DEVELOPMENT PLAN

Based on the mentoring agenda, you can work out or prescribe a personal development plan for the mentee's learning focus. It is better if the mentee can create a development plan under the guidance of the mentor. The mentor would then hold the mentee accountable to what they determined for themselves. Depending on the individual mentee, it may be necessary for the mentor to prescribe a development plan. As much as possible, find ways to frame the discussion around the plan so that the mentee can buy in and take ownership of the learning.

In ministry mentoring, the mentee's character development and spiritual growth are inevitability a part of the mentoring agenda. An indirect approach may be best for this aspect of the agenda. Mentees will need to embrace the disciplines that lead to spiritual formation and character transformation. Dallas Willard says, "In general, a discipline is any activity within our power that we engage in to enable us to do what we cannot do by direct effort."[102] The mentor may suggest various spiritual disciplines which, when combined with the appropriation of God's grace, will result in the desired development outcomes.

Another character development strategy which should not be underestimated is the power of example. When possible, the mentor should be intentional about inviting mentees into multiple life and ministry contexts.

---

102 Dallas Willard, *Renewing the Christian Mind: Essays, Interviews, and Talks* (New York, NY: Harper Collins, 2016), 32.

Here they will have opportunities to observe the mentor modelling character and spiritual life.

For instance, a picture that sticks with me from the early days of ministry is that of regularly kneeling in prayer together with my father at the front pew of the church. We sought God's blessing there for the congregation and his direction in ministry. Creating memories like this will make indelible impressions on the mentee and shape their character.

WHAT IS THE LEARNING STYLE OF THE MENTEE?

Learning activities, whenever possible, should be planned to take into account the preferred learning style of the mentee. One theory suggests that people fall into four learning style categories: activist, reflector, theorist, and pragmatist.[103] Learning activities include variations of doing, watching, thinking, and feeling. These are part of a cycle of learning that the learner—in this case, the mentee—touches at the different stages of the learning journey. Learning activities can be planned accordingly. Klasen and Clutterbuck suggest,

> For mentors to be successful in developing their mentees, it helps to know a mentee's learning style and adjust their developmental efforts to these. Adapting to the mentee's learning style means helping the mentee to identify those learning opportunities from which he or she is likely to benefit most.[104]

Here is a table that outlines the different learning styles and how they operate.

---

[103] Klasen and Clutterbuck, 173. The model described here is developed by P. Honey and A. Mumford, based on D. Kolb's experiential learning theory. There are several theories of learning style, but it is not within the scope of this book to describe them all. For a mentoring relationship, simply taking into account the existence of learning styles will enable the mentor to adapt the learning experience.

[104] Ibid., 174.

Learning style	Process	Learning preference
Activist	do and feel	Doing and experiencing the ministry activity
Reflector	watch and feel	Observing someone else do the ministry activity and review what happened
Theorist	think and watch	Developing models and theories about the ministry activity and see how they work as others do them
Pragmatist	think and do	Planning a ministry activity, learning what is needed at the moment and trying it out

Table 2: Learning Styles Overview

While these categories are helpful, the mentor should not be overly concerned if the mentee's preference is not clear. However, the mentor will likely already know into which category the mentee fits based on the mentor's interaction with the mentee. In any case, the mentee will need to employ several, if not all, the learning styles at different phases of the critical growth pathways to embrace fully what needs to be learned. The benefit of identifying the learning style is to determine the best entry point in the learning cycle so that the mentee is motivated at the beginning.

For instance, Bill is an activist. He doesn't need a second invitation to preach, even if he has never done it. Bill wants to learn by doing. He wants to feel what preaching is like. He has absorbed some of the knowledge and skills from his mentor, but he may not be able to explain them. He is not likely to reflect on how the experience went unless he is compelled in some way. The mentor will need to find ways to guide him into other learning processes.

Karen is a reflector. She prefers to watch someone preach and then talk with her mentor about what she saw. Eventually, she will also need to plan her own sermon and preach it, so that she can experience what it is like. To complete the cycle of learning, Karen will need to think about and develop her own theory (or model) of preaching.

David, on the other hand, is a pragmatist. He prefers to be asked to preach and then think briefly about the best way to do it. David will consider several methods that are close at hand and then test one of them. He will learn what works from experience and adjust his plan to do even better next time. He doesn't like to watch from the sidelines, but his mentor may need to ask him to pause and reflect on the big picture so that his learning experience can be augmented.

Barbara is a theorist. She loves to analyze the sermons and delivery styles of others when they preach. Barbara will be able to theorize why one sermon is better than another and develop theories on the best way to preach. But she will be very reluctant to do it. She will need a high motivation to put her thoughts into action.

These examples may remind you of people you know, but in real life all of us have needed to learn through styles other than our preferred style. Which one often depends on the skill we need to acquire. Some skills aren't learnable through the mentee's preferred style. The mentee will adapt. They are motivated because of their felt need to learn the skill. Thus, where possible, the mentor should design the learning activity to fit the preferred learning style of mentee. But the mentee will also need to engage other learning styles. It is helpful to understand the theory behind the skill as well as to get the feel and experience of engaging in the skill. It is as important to reflect on the impact of the ministry activity as it is to make it work well.

These other questions may help you adapt the way you facilitate the learning of the mentees:

- What are their working styles?
- What are their leadership styles?
- What does their learning journey look like up to this point?
- Where are they on their spiritual journey?

In these last two chapters, we have considered who the mentee is and how to identify the things they need in order to grow at this point in their life and ministry. In this chapter, we have tried to determine the mentoring agenda (what they need to learn) and the critical growth pathways (how they will learn it). In the next chapter, we will describe how to become intentional about engaging them by creating a mentoring agreement.

QUESTIONS: FROM REFLECTION TO ACTION

1. Explain from your own experience why character development should take priority over the development of ministry skills.
2. Take an example of a ministry skill in your own skillset and describe it in terms of basic skill, contextual application, and strategic implementation.
3. What is the difference between the mentoring agenda and the learning development plan? How do you move from one to the other?
4. What is your learning style, based on the description of learning styles in this chapter?

Chapter Ten

BEING INTENTIONAL—THE MENTORING AGREEMENT

CHARLES WAS A POPULAR PASTOR IN HIS CITY. YOUNGER PASTORS WOULD SEEK him out and ask him to mentor them, and he would agree to do so. But he soon discerned a pattern. Some just wanted to spend time visiting and others wanted to ask him about how he did ministry. Some wanted to meet regularly and others just called up spontaneously and asked if he was available for coffee.

Charles didn't mind spending time with these younger pastors, but he wondered how effective his mentoring really was. Undoubtedly he was a blessing to them, and they certainly felt affirmed and encouraged whenever they met with him. But there didn't seem to be a way to evaluate whether any of these pastors learned anything.

He wanted his mentoring to be purposeful, so he decided to become more intentional about his encounters by making mentoring agreements with those who were prepared to commit to such arrangements. He still connected with others informally from time to time, but the formal mentoring agreements enabled Charles to prioritize his time with those who really wanted to learn from him.

In this chapter, we will describe how we can make a mentoring agreement, but first we want to share a little more about the nature of the relationship that is in view.

THE NATURE OF THE MENTORING RELATIONSHIP

The mentoring model of this book assumes mentorship to be an intentional learning relationship which is mentee-driven and mentor-guided. In his book on *Relational Leadership*, Walter Wright states:

> Mentoring is a relationship with a purpose. There is no formula, no ideal model, and no program of steps to success. It is a relationship connected by a shared interest in learning and growth, and it must be constantly nurtured and recreated. It has purpose and structure defined by the learning needs of the mentoree and shaped by the wisdom and experience of the mentor.[105]

He goes on to say that "mentoring is a leadership relationship in which both the mentor and mentoree add value and benefit, but at its core, mentoring is a relationship of learning directed by the mentoree."[106] This definition of mentoring assumes a high level of maturity on the part of the mentor, as well as that of the mentee. It also assumes a cultural environment where social conventions allow for leaders and their followers to interact more or less as equals.

As I mentioned when discussing reverse mentoring, a mentoring relationship such as this adds value to the mentor who, as a lifelong learner, can greatly benefit as he or she interacts with a mentee. The mentor is as open to learning in the context of the mentoring relationship as the mentee is.

Mentoring in such a context also includes vulnerable sharing by the mentor. In some cultural contexts, the power distance between leaders and followers, or mentors and mentees, is higher than in other settings. Such vulnerability on the part of the mentor may potentially create awkwardness for the mentor or mentee, especially in the early phases of the relationship. Some adaptation to the approach is necessary to reduce such awkwardness. Johnson and Ridley note that "some protégés hold personally rigid or

---

105 Walter C. Wright, Jr., *Mentoring: The Promise of Relational Leadership* (Waynesboro, GA: Paternoster, 2004), 68.
106 Ibid., 72.

culturally hierarchal views of seniors. For these protégés, collegiality with a supervisor is destabilizing and disorienting...In these cases, mentors have to be sensitive to the needs of the protégé."[107]

Learner-centred mentoring represents a relatively recent trend where mentees actively participate in setting their own learning agenda. In *The Mentor's Guide*, Zachary promotes a learner-centred paradigm of mentoring and describes it as a learning partnership. She describes the relationship this way:

> The learner—in this case, the mentee—plays an active role in the learning, sharing responsibility for the priorities, learning, and resources, and becoming increasingly self-directed in the process. The mentor nurtures and develops the mentee's capacity for self-direction (from dependence to independence to interdependence) over the course of the relationship. Throughout the learning relationship, both mentoring partners share accountability and responsibility for achieving the mentee's learning goals.[108]

In this paradigm are "seven critical elements: reciprocity, learning, relationship, partnership, collaboration, mutually defined goals, and development."[109] Note that five of the seven terms to denote these elements indicate a profound sense of interconnectedness between the mentor and mentee. Reciprocity refers to the give-and-take nature of the mentoring relationship which benefits both parties. Learning refers to the goal of the mentoring relationship in which the mentee is the learner, and the mentor is the learning facilitator who creates a learning environment. The elements of relationship, partnership, and collaboration all highlight the need for trust, agreement, and consensus respectively between the mentor and mentee as they work on mutually defined goals that lead to the development of the mentee's knowledge, thinking, and skills.

---

107 Johnson and Ridley, 41–2.
108 Zachary, location 476.
109 Ibid., location 484.

Since the mentee actively participates in, and ultimately needs to take ownership of, the learning that occurs in a mentoring relationship, it makes sense for them to develop skills which enable them to make the most of such a relationship. They need to know what role they should play and what they can expect. For instance, one book that addresses prospective mentees makes the following suggestion to them:

> Before you can engage with a mentor, you need to do some serious and focused preparation that will help you know better what you want to achieve, how you learn best, and what kind of mentoring relationship might work well for you.[110]

Chapter Eleven addresses this in more detail, providing suggestions for how mentees can make the most of a mentoring relationship.

In formal mentoring relationships, there are seasons (or phases) over the lifetime of the relationship. We can see these by comparing the way different mentoring experts have expressed them.

	BEGINNINGS		CORE LEARNING	ENDINGS	
A	Building Rapport	Setting Direction	Progression	Winding Up	Moving On
B	Preparing	Negotiating	Enabling Growth	Coming to Closure	
C	Initiation		Cultivation	Separation	Redefinition

Table 3: Comparing Different Expressions of Mentorship Phases

---

110 Lois J. Zachary and Lory A. Fischler, *The Mentee's Guide: Making Mentoring Work for You*, first edition, The Jossey-Bass Higher and Adult Education Series (San Francisco, CA: Jossey-Bass, 2009), 15.

In Row A, there are five phases: building rapport, setting direction, progression, winding up, and moving on.[111] In Row B, four phases are outlined: preparing, negotiating, enabling growth, and coming to closure.[112] And Row C suggests four phases: initiation, cultivation, separation, and redefinition.[113]

As is seen in the table, these phases correspond to the *beginnings* of a mentoring relationship, the period during which *core learning* takes place in the relationship, and the endings of a mentoring relationship. However these phases are named, they are predictable. As you begin to negotiate a mentoring agreement, it is helpful to be aware of these. This awareness can help both the mentor and mentee adapt to the changes that occur during the lifetime of the relationship. Understanding this dynamic and planning with this in mind is part of what makes the mentoring relationship intentional.

The relationship can be structured according to the needs of the mentee and the availability of the mentor. Some mentoring relationships may require a greater investment of time and emotional energy, and others less. Some of that needs to be worked out at the beginning of the relationship when the ground rules and expectations are negotiated. These would be included in a mentoring agreement that provides clarity for the mentoring relationship.

We'll now look at some of the things to consider when beginning an intentional formal mentoring relationship.

BEGINNING A MENTORING RELATIONSHIP

Some of the questions to ponder as you begin a mentoring relationship have already been mentioned, but I've included them here as a part of a checklist with further comments:

- How was the connection with the mentee made?
- Did you select the mentee?

---

111 David Clutterbuck, "Mentor Competences: A Field Perspective," in *The Situational Mentor: An International Review of Competencies and Capabilities in Mentoring*, ed. David Clutterbuck and Gill Lane (Burlington, VT: Gower, 2004), 44–5.
112 Zachary, location 2449.
113 Johnson and Ridley, 96–97.

- Did the mentee request to be mentored by you?
- Were you connected through a mentoring program or an initiative by your organization?

The way the mentor and mentee made their initial connection will have an impact on the intrinsic motivations that will sustain the mentoring relationship. The mentor and mentee will both need to reflect on who and what drives the relationship. Being aware of that will enable them to put structures in place that will give their relationship the best chance of success.

- Have you prayed about whether you should be mentoring this person?
- Is this the right time?

As mentioned earlier, selecting a mentee involves prayer on the part of the mentor so that the mentee can be in alignment with the priorities of the Holy Spirit in their life, in their emerging ministry, and the purposes of the kingdom of God. The mentor also needs to be aware of his personal season of life, ministry schedule, and workload.

- Is there a supervisory obligation in the relationship?
- Is there any financial issue connected to the relationship? Is there a way to remove finances from the relationship (for example, by delegating the matter to a church board)?
- What are your motives in this relationship?

There may be a mixture of motives, such as wanting to help the mentee grow or getting someone to help in certain areas of ministry. These are not bad motives, but the mentor needs to be aware of them and make sure that their priority is the mentee's best interests in particular and the kingdom of God in general. Another motive may be the sense of fulfillment and satisfaction that comes from helping someone in ministry leadership.

It's important to clarify the expectations on the mentoring relationships from all sides.

Expectations of the Mentee

Are you aware of all the expectations that the mentee may have, spoken and unspoken? These could include:

- The mentor will spend time with them in discussion.
- The mentor will provide learning opportunities, perhaps through college or in-church training.
- The mentor will arrange on-the-job practical opportunities.
- The mentor will assign ministry responsibilities.
- The mentor will coach them through ministry assignments.
- The mentor will cover ministry expenses, if applicable.

And finally, as the mentor, ask the mentee what he or she hopes to gain from the mentoring relationship. Be sure to clarify to the mentee what you are prepared to include as part of the mentoring agreement so that he or she will not have unwarranted expectations.

Expectations of the Mentor

If the mentee is being mentored in the context of ministry, and if the mentor is responsible for the outcome, the mentor will find himself in the position of having to balance the development goals of the mentee and the objectives of ministry. The mentor will need to be clear on what the priorities are as the relationship progresses. The mentee will also need to be made aware of those priorities from time to time.

If the mentoring relationship is separate from ministry objectives, the focus can be placed on the mentee's development needs. The expectations of the mentor, then, will be primarily to see growth in the mentee. These are some of the expectations the mentor will have:

- The mentee is willing to learn.
- The mentee is willing to submit to basic rules and instructions relating to the mentoring relationship and ministry context.

- The mentee is willing to schedule regular meeting times, either one-on-one or group mentoring times, as applicable.
- The mentee is willing to actively participate in a ministry context which includes opportunities for growth.

Beyond these expectations, ask yourself as the mentor, "What am I hoping for from the relationship?"

Expectations in the Ministry Context

This section assumes that there may be other stakeholders in the mentoring relationship. If this applies, ask the following questions:

- What is the church or organization expecting from this relationship?
- Does anyone else have expectations in this relationship? (For example, another pastor or Bible college.)

Learning Goals and Objectives

The mentor and mentee should both agree on the learning objectives of the mentoring arrangement, including the mentoring agenda and critical growth pathways. These can be evaluated and amended from time to time. A development plan with specific learning activities should be outlined.

Other Matters to Discuss with the Mentee

As the development plan is being set, there are several other things you may consider discussing with the mentee that will give shape to the mentoring agreement. Here is a list of questions that can guide you, but there are possibly other things you may need to ask depending on your context.

- What are the rules and boundaries in the relationship?
- Speak about matters of confidentiality.
- When and how often will you meet one-on-one?

- Does the mentee have other people in their life who have a mentoring-like role in their life and ministry? (This is not a bad thing, but you need to be aware of this.)
- What is the mentee's awareness of their call to ministry?
- Set a specific time when you will review the relationship (perhaps in three months).
- How long will you continue in this mentoring relationship? (There is no need to fix a date of conclusion at the outset, but establish the fact that a formal mentoring relationship will eventually conclude, though it may continue as an informal relationship or friendship.)

General Considerations

At this point in the process, before making a final commitment to an agreement, it may be a good idea for the mentor to step back and examine this prospective mentorship from a broader perspective by asking the following questions:

- How will having a mentee impact the mentor's life and ministry?
- Is there anything that concerns the mentor about the mentee? (If so, how will those concerns be addressed?)
- The mentor needs to ask if they are the best person available to mentor this mentee at this time. (If yes, they should go for it. If not, they should prayerfully consider helping the mentee connect with someone else.)

SETTING DIRECTION AND NEGOTIATING A DEVELOPMENT PLAN

In the process of working out the mentoring agreement, the mentor and mentee must discuss the first draft of their development plan. Appendix B provides an example of what such an agreement might look like. The development plan flows out of the critical growth pathways, which are based on the mentoring agenda. Figure 8 illustrates the process of how learning objectives are determined in an intentional mentoring relationship.

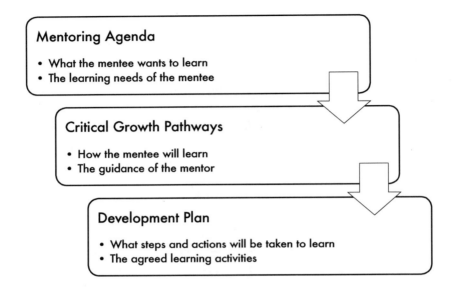

Figure 8: Determining the Learning Objective of the Mentee

In the development plan, specific growth goals and objectives are identified, and corresponding learning activities are proposed for the next several weeks. These can be adapted as the mentor and mentee get to know one another better. It is best if the mentee clearly indicates what their goals are, but sometimes, depending on the maturity level and experience of the mentee, the mentor may need to take the initiative to make some suggestions.

If people in the ministry organization initiate the mentoring relationship, they may have already set some development goals with implications for how the mentee will continue to relate to the organization. The mentor may also have a mentoring model that he or she may like to follow, which will give shape to the development plan. For instance, in ministry mentoring it is best to work on spiritual matters and character since effective Christian ministry flows from healthy spiritual foundations.

The development plan may include activities that the mentor assigns the mentee, such as reading, research, seminars, workshops, and courses or development projects which will enhance the mentee's learning. The plan will include regular meetings to discuss, debrief, and deliver feedback. It may also include the mentee observing the mentor in a ministry activity or participating together in team ministry activities, followed by a discussion. The mentee may connect with other mentors related to specific development objectives as a part of the plan.

In Chapter Nine, we saw how the content of core learning is determined. From time to time during the core learning phase, the learning of the mentee needs to be evaluated in light of the development plan. The mentor and mentee make course corrections so that the mentoring relationship can stay on track and fulfill its intended purpose.

Randy was one of the pastors who asked Charles to mentor him. He wanted to learn how to train lay leaders more effectively in his congregation. Charles asked him what purpose the training of leaders would serve, and Randy replied that he needed people to help him in dealing with pastoral issues because he wasn't able to keep up with the congregation's demands.

"Then who would the leaders be leading?" Charles asked. "And how would that be structured?"

He asked this to help Randy clarify why he needed the leaders, but also to help Randy begin to think strategically. The discussion landed on how the congregation was structured and they agreed that the solution would require more than Randy learning how to train leaders to deal with pastoral issues. He would have to learn a whole new way to do church, a way which involved having small groups that were led by leaders who could be trained. Charles also discerned that Randy had difficulty trusting people to do their jobs. He tended to micromanage. He suspected that this may have made it difficult for the potential leaders in Randy's congregation to fully embrace their responsibilities.

Thus, the mentoring agenda became about Randy learning to train leaders. The critical growth pathways would require Randy to think about how the church needed to be restructured, and then to train, release, and empower leaders to manage small groups. But these pathways also involved Charles helping Randy to learn how to trust others, a character issue that Charles would have to deal with at a spiritual level.

The development plan that Charles and Randy negotiated involved several aspects, including learning activities that would have Randy sit in on some of the meetings Charles had with his leaders. Randy would have to read books on small-group-based church models, attend seminars and debriefing meetings, and make plans to engage the church's current leadership. Charles also recommended a personality assessment, to generate discussion concerning Randy's leadership style and trust issues.

These learning objectives and specific learning activities became a part of the mentoring agreement. Charles agreed to mentor Randy through a season, transitioning his church to a model in which well-trained leaders led small groups and dealt with pastoral care issues in the small group context.

CONCLUDING A FORMAL MENTORING RELATIONSHIP

One of the things an intentional mentoring relationship has in its favour is that it can be structured to include closure. Many mentoring relationships just fade away without acknowledgment. Even though the actual purpose of the mentorship was achieved, there often remains the feeling of unfinished business simply because the mentorship was not brought to a formal conclusion. When the mentor and mentee understand from the outset that there will be an ending to their arrangement, it is much easier to bring the relationship to a satisfying end, or at least to a clearly recognized transition. They may have a final meeting and say goodbye, or they may leave the door open to informal mentoring encounters as needed. It's not unusual for a lifelong friendship to follow. This is also an opportunity to celebrate the milestone of a successfully executed mentorship where learning objectives were achieved.

It is also entirely possible for a mentoring relationship to conclude before its goals are fulfilled. Life changes can happen midstream that make it difficult to continue the relationship. Unforeseen compatibility issues between the mentor and mentee may emerge early in the relationship. Whatever the reason for ending the mentorship, it is best to find a way to bring it to a definite and formal conclusion so that both mentor and mentee can move on to minimize the potential for awkwardness.

SUMMARY

To summarize, the mentoring agreement should include the following points:

- The suggested duration of the mentorship, with options to shorten or lengthen it.
- A mutual understanding of what the conclusion might look like.
- Meeting times and other means of staying in touch, including levels of accessibility to the mentor.
- Scheduled times to evaluate progress and satisfaction with the relationship.
- Potential challenges to the interaction and how these will be handled.
- A development plan with goals and objectives (with the option to amend them as needed during evaluation times).
- Expectations that the mentor and mentee have of each other.
- How any confidential matters will be handled.
- What the role of the mentee's ministry supervisors might take in the relationship.

Whenever possible, a document should be drawn up to include these and any other points of agreement. When both the mentor and mentee sign such a document, it helps to formalize the relationship and strengthen the accountability factor. The mentor may have a mentoring agreement template to assist and clarify what an agreement entails. In some cultural contexts, a written agreement may seem out of place, or even intimidating. If that's the case, simply having a discussion concerning the points mentioned, with a verbal commitment expressed by both the mentor and mentee, can constitute a mentoring agreement.[114]

---

114 Sometimes asking the mentee to make notes of the points of agreement reduces the intimidation factor.

In concluding this section, I would like to encourage mentors to take the time to understand the spirit behind the methods, principles, steps, and agreements. The mechanisms should be learned well so they can fade into the background and not become a distraction. The focus throughout needs to remain on the learning objectives as well as the relational aspects of the mentorship.

QUESTIONS: FROM REFLECTION TO ACTION

1. Why do think it is important for the mentee to set the learning agenda? How is that different from a school setting?
2. What do you see as the primary value of a mentoring agreement?
3. What current mentorships are you engaged in that would benefit from a formal mentoring agreement? How would you start a discussion with your mentee about it?
4. What are some practical considerations concerning mentoring agreements? Are there some situations in which oral agreements may work better? What is the benefit of a written agreement?

Chapter Eleven

A WORD FOR THE MENTEE

IN THIS BOOK, I HAVE PRIMARILY ADDRESSED MENTORS. IN THIS CHAPTER, I would like to direct some thoughts toward potential mentees. Most people who start out in a new job or ministry role are inclined to welcome someone who's willing and able to help them through the challenges of a new context. Some things cannot be learned in a classroom or from a book. Not even an internet search will provide the knowledge, wisdom, or skills required to navigate some situations. For that reason, this book promotes the multiplication of ministry mentors who have the relational skills and knowledge to effectively mentor those who are at the earlier stages of their ministry journeys.

WHY DO I NEED A MENTOR?

The answer to the question "Why do I need a mentor?" is self-evident to most people who want to grow in their life and ministry. It is nonetheless a good exercise to review some of the benefits of a mentoring relationship. A good mentor will encourage and nurture your growth as a person, minister, and leader. They will provide correction and discipline in a safe environment. You will be in a better position to watch them through direct observation as they model their ministry behaviour and skills, and you'll be able to ask how they do what they do and why they do as they do. You will have access to many of the stories of their learning journey.

Some of the things you have learned in a school setting, you can translate into practical reality with the help of a mentor. A mentor will guide you in the appropriate use of your natural abilities, acquired skills, and spiritual gifts in the ministries to which you have been called. Indeed, a mentor may even help you clarify your calling. Naomi Dowdy, who has been a mentor to me and many others, writes:

> Especially in ministry settings, having a mentor to walk with you and help you mature in your ministry will allow you to fail without doubting God's call. It will also help you learn from your mistakes as you walk with someone who has the experience, wisdom, and ability to help you grow and develop. Proper alignment with a mentor is not only a great source of guidance and support; it can also be crucial to the fulfillment of your destiny and vital to your getting to the next level.[115]

WHAT HAPPENS IN A MENTORING RELATIONSHIP?

A mentoring relationship provides a safe environment to have conversations about your life and ministry. A good mentor will not only be interested in the development of your ministry skills and leadership journey, but also your spiritual, emotional, intellectual, and physical health. Growth and development in all these areas will have an impact on the sustainability of a successful ministry. In these conversations, your mentor will ask questions that invite you to reflect on all the areas of your life and how you can take steps to move you toward an effective ministry in the roles God has designed for you to play in his kingdom. Sometimes the mentor will impart ministry wisdom based on his or her experience, perhaps helping you to avoid pitfalls and unnecessary detours.

Occasionally there will be opportunities to observe the mentor in ministry contexts where you can learn by watching and then ask follow-up questions. There may even be opportunities for the hands-on practice of new ministry skills, followed by an evaluation and debriefing. The opportunity for hands-on practice may simply be part of the ministry context in

---

115 Naomi Dowdy, *Moving On and Moving Up: Ten Practical Principles for Getting to the Next Level* (Dallas, TX: Naomi Dowdy Ministries, 2006), 54.

which you already work, only now with a mentor to guide you toward a better learning outcome. Processing these experiences with your mentor will enable you to pay attention to those things which are important and be less anxious about peripheral issues.

An effective mentor will encourage and correct you as needed. You will be able to "test drive" your ministry dreams and visions with someone who has had life experience. In the areas in which your mentor doesn't have expertise, she may be able to connect you with people and learning resources you can access and process with her so you may learn new things together. A mentor will also be able to help you set growth goals that challenge but not overwhelm you. As the mentoring relationship continues, you will observe growth in yourself and gain confidence in the areas of ministry in which you aspire to excel.

HOW CAN I FIND THE RIGHT MENTOR?[116]

Mentors and mentees make the mentoring connection in different ways. Sometimes the mentee takes the initiative and approaches a potential mentor and asks if he is available to be a mentor. Sometimes it is the mentor who takes the initiative and invites a mentee to discuss the possibilities of a mentoring relationship. Some organizations have intentional programs that match mentors and mentees as part of their overall strategy of leadership development.

Often the ministry context puts people into a working relationship which inevitably includes mentoring. Usually, that means the mentor is also a ministry supervisor. For example, a lead pastor may hire an assistant to fulfill a particular role on the ministry staff. If the assistant is less experienced as a minister, mentoring activities will undoubtedly be a part of learning the required ministry skills, particularly in the beginning.

If you pray for what you need in a mentor, the Lord will direct you to the right person. However, you may not always know what is best. Just as it

---

116 Some of the points in this section have been adapted from the chapter entitlted "How to Find a Mentor" in Howard G. Hendricks and William Hendricks, *As Iron Sharpens Iron: Building Character in a Mentoring Relationship* (Chicago, IL: Moody Press, 1995), 73–84.

is in other areas of life, trust that the Lord will help you find someone who participates in your learning journey in a meaningful way.

Keep your eyes open and carefully observe the life and ministry skills of your potential mentor. Ask yourself what you need in a mentor and seek out a mentor who has those characteristics.

- Does this mentor have the ability to cultivate relationships?
- Is this mentor willing to take a chance on investing their time with you?
- Do they have the respect of others in Christian circles?
- Who else consults them?
- What is their reputation?
- Do they know how to listen to people, or do they only talk a lot?
- Do they only listen and not say much, or do they know when to speak up at appropriate times?
- Are they consistent in their lifestyle?
- Do they demonstrate the heart of a mentor, concerned about the needs of the mentee?
- Do they also know how to balance those needs with the priorities of the kingdom of God?

Be aware that you aren't likely to find the perfect mentor or someone who meets all your criteria. However, creating a checklist of the points mentioned, among others you may add, will identify a set of standards to help you find the person most suited to your learning needs.

Note also that mentors come in all personality types and will have different mentoring styles. Some mentors will share their knowledge, skills, and wisdom with a little prodding. Others will require more direct questions to get what you need from them. The best mentors will be guides for your learning journey, leading you in a way that helps you make your own discoveries whenever possible.

When you have identified someone you think could be a good mentor for you, arrange to have a conversation with him or her to see if you have the right connection for a mentoring relationship. If so, ask if they are willing to consider being your mentor. Be ready to share the reasons you would like to be mentored by them. Give them the opportunity to think and pray about it and set a time to follow up with them and begin the process of negotiating a mentoring agreement.

It is possible that even though they may be excellent mentors, they may not have the same understanding of mentoring that you have. Take time to discuss what you mean by a mentoring relationship. Give them a copy of this book or at least a summary of mentoring as you have come to understand it.

HOW CAN I MAKE THE MOST OF A MENTORING RELATIONSHIP?

As a mentee, you must take responsibility for your learning. The mentor is not responsible for that. You are the one who seeks out the knowledge, skills, and wisdom for the ministry to which God has called you. So while the mentor may guide you in setting up the critical growth pathways for your learning journey, you need to work at receiving what the mentor has to give and diligently explore those areas that will be most helpful in making you the minister and leader you aspire to be.

Observe your mentor's life and ministry and take the best examples from what you see and follow those. There may also be some areas which are not good examples and may not be appropriate for you to follow. Learn from both your mentor's successes and failures. Let the mentor take the lead in discussing shortfalls in his or her life—at least at the beginning of the mentoring relationship. As the trust level in the relationship increases, the mentor may be open for you to inquire about some of those difficult areas.

Prepare yourself for the mentoring times. Be ready with questions and fulfill any assignments given at previous meetings. Do not let the mentor feel that time spent with you is wasted. Be determined to show progress. For most mentors, observable growth in their mentees is all the reward they need to stay motivated and fully engaged in the mentoring relationship.

Take your mentor's advice seriously. When you know that a mentor has your interest in mind, she will try to give you advice based on lessons she has learned (sometimes the hard way, by mistakes she has made). Your mentor doesn't want you to suffer unnecessarily. If you choose not to follow such advice, ensure that you have good reasons which you can clearly articulate. It may not be a deal-breaker, but nothing is as disheartening to a mentor as when a mentee repeatedly ignores the wise advice that comes from experience.

Respect your mentor in the manner that is appropriate in your culture and his or her culture. Mentors have gone before their mentees in their ministry journey and invite mentees to learn from them. Mentees can build on this previous knowledge and experience, and sometimes even surpass their mentors in certain areas. The mentee, in such cases, will do well to remember to honour and respect mentors who have contributed to their development and ministry success.

Some things the mentor shares with you should be kept confidential. The mentor will invite you to ponder some things from his life and ministry which are private and intended only for your learning and not to be shared further. If in doubt, ask. It may be that a certain ministry scenario you are participating in involves other people's private matters. You must keep these matters confidential and follow all the rules of ministerial ethics, even if it happens as a part of your learning journey.

Learn how to trust your mentor. It is important, of course, that your mentor also earn your trust. This may take time. But to the degree that you feel comfortable, be as open to your mentor as you can about your life and ministry. As the mentoring relationship allows for mutual trust, share with your mentor your fears, struggles, and frustrations. As you discuss these matters, your mentor will be able to guide you prayerfully along critical growth pathways that strengthen you.

At times, your mentor may disappoint you in some way. If possible, engage them in an honest conversation concerning the disappointment. Such engagement is critical since a continued feeling of being let down will undermine the mentoring relationship. If you have that difficult conversation, you may discover backstories which help you to see the situation in a better light. Or you may assist the mentor with a shortcoming of which they were not aware. It may not be as easy as this explanation sounds, but it is better to say something than to ignore it. In any case, your disappointment does not give you license to speak ill of the mentor to others.[117]

If you have more than one mentor, identify who your primary mentor is and make a habit of asking him to help you process the input from other mentors. When you engage in conversation with different mentors, you may find that their advice is not always in perfect alignment. In some cases, the advice you receive from one may contradict the advice from another. It may simply be that they each have their own perspectives. Your primary mentor can be the sounding board where you can discover what direction to take concerning a particular matter.

In conclusion, pray for your mentor, bless your mentor, and find ways to show appreciation for your mentor. Also, be a mentor to someone else and be the link that transfers living faith and empowered ministry from preceding mentoring generations to your mentee. The apostle Paul wrote to Timothy,

> *And the things you have heard me say in the presence of many witnesses entrust to reliable people who will also be qualified to teach others.*
> —2 Timothy 2:2

QUESTIONS: FROM REFLECTION TO ACTION

1. If you are a mentor, are you being mentored by anyone?
2. What kind of learning relationships do you currently have in your life?
3. Where have you been looking for a mentor? How have you gone about looking for a mentor?
4. What do you want to learn from a mentor that you cannot learn from anyone else?
5. What is your next step?

---

117 Note that if the mentoring relationship is part of a mentoring program in an organization, the mentoring coordinator can be invited to help facilitate the awkward conversation.

Chapter Twelve
NAVIGATING CHALLENGES IN MINISTRY MENTORING

MINISTRY MENTORING IS AN ART RATHER THAN A PRECISE SCIENCE. THOUGH WE outline steps, map out procedures, and create checklists, the mentor will need to be aware of subtleties and nuances that can emerge in the various situations of a mentoring relationship.

Mentoring relationships, in any case, have their share of potential issues which may require special attention. I would like to address some of these issues in this chapter so the mentor can be equipped to deal with them. Some may seem like common sense, but it is nonetheless helpful to state these issues and suggest possible ways to navigate them.

I begin with one issue we have already discussed—namely, when the mentor is also in a supervisory relationship with the mentee.

SUPERVISORY RELATIONSHIPS AND MENTORING

Many mentoring relationships in a ministry context flow naturally from a supervisory relationship. This can work well provided that the dual roles of mentor and supervisor are clearly understood. In the supervisor role, the minister focuses on ministry objectives. The subordinate who is also the mentee receives directives, takes on responsibilities, and is answerable to the supervising minister. The dynamic may be somewhat different if the mentee is part of a team and team members hold each other accountable, but the focus is nonetheless on fulfilling ministry objectives. In the mentor role, the supervising minister focuses on the development of the mentee.

The mentee receives encouragement, affirmation, and other input from the mentor to help them grow as a person and minister.

A key factor that can make this dual role arrangement work is the mindset of the supervising minister. The minister needs to see the mentee as one who seeks to grow in character, ministry skills, and leadership. The mentee should not be considered a mere employee or volunteer who fulfills ministry responsibilities. In general, mentees need to be seen not only for what they can contribute in the present but also for how they can be developed for their roles in future ministry. In their book *Deep Mentoring*, Reese and Loane suggest that

> there is a need for a subtle but critical paradigm shift—moving from an *enlisting way* of ministering in our communities to more of an *investing way* of ministering. So much of our leadership culture is dominated by the need to enlist volunteers for the various activities of the church... The work of enlisting others will always be part of our leadership culture, but what if our primary attention was given to people investment?[118]

As mentioned previously, the mentor should make a conscious effort to clearly state when he is wearing his "mentor hat" and when he is wearing the "boss hat." This is more important at the beginning of the relationship as the mentor and mentee establish lines of communication. As the relationship develops, this clarification will not need to be mentioned as often.

While the dual role can work in most cases, in some scenarios it is best for a mentoring relationship to take place outside of the supervisory context. The mentee may not be comfortable expressing some things to a supervisor and would rather have a mentor who is not a direct supervisor.[119] If that is the case, where possible the supervisory and mentor roles should be delinked and the mentee should seek out a mentoring relationship outside of his or her reporting line. However this is achieved, it is important

---

118 Reese and Loane, 20–21.
119 For instance, this may be the case in a situation where the mentee is in an employee, and employment and salary structure are connected to performance reviews.

that the mentee communicate this to the ministry supervisor to avoid misunderstandings.

THE ISSUE OF MIXED GENDER MENTORSHIPS

In almost every place I have taught about ministry mentoring, invariably someone asks about mixed gender mentoring. My short answer is that mentoring relationships normally should be between people of the same sex. It's simpler and safer to say that, but ministry isn't always straightforward.

In some cultural contexts, this is more of an issue than in others. We nonetheless observe, even in some of the stricter cultural backgrounds, that ministries such as counselling happen across gender lines. There are usually appropriate measures in place to avoid wrong perceptions and safeguard against temptations.

But Scripture does provide principles to consider as we try to navigate this issue. It is clear that men and women are one in Christ, partners in ministry, and co-heirs (Galatians 3:28–29 and Romans 16:3). Spiritual gifts have been distributed to sons and daughters alike for ministry (Acts 2:17–18). For the apostle Paul, there was nothing unusual about men and women relating together in ministry contexts, but proprieties were to be observed (1 Timothy 5:1–2).

However, we need to acknowledge that we live in a broken world (1 John 2:15–17). Our human desires sometimes run at cross-purposes with our best intentions (Romans 7:18–20). We remain targets of our enemy, the devil (Ephesians 6:11 and 1 Peter 5:8). Because of these factors, mentoring relationships between members of the opposite sex can become the object of mistaken perceptions to people in the community. And we must not underestimate the real potential of inappropriate emotional and sexual attraction.[120]

With these biblical principles in view, let us establish some guidelines for mentoring between men and women. I recommend that the default

---

120 Note for instance: "The area in which mentors should be most careful pertains to emotional and sexual attraction. Research in many professions reveals the existence of sexualized male-mentor female-protégé relationships" (Johnson and Ridley, 81).

arrangement for one-on-one mentorships be men mentoring men and women mentoring women. We should nonetheless make ample room for the possibility of mixed gender mentorships because there are many good reasons for men and women to share in ministry mentorships. One such possibility is group mentorships where both males and females can be in a mentoring relationship with a mentor. Some one-on-one mentoring can be part of the arrangement, with safeguards in place as necessary.

Another possibility is where there is a significant age difference between the mentor and the mentee, though in certain cases the right precautions are still in order. Yet another scenario is when the mentor and mentee are married to other people. In such a case, the spouses should be aware of, and if possible included in, some aspects of the mentorship. If any of the spouses become uncomfortable or feel awkward about the mentoring relationship, it should either be modified to mitigate the awkwardness or concluded. When singles initiate a mixed gender mentoring relationship, we would expect proper measures to be taken to prevent undesirable outcomes.

Safeguards in these scenarios could include clearly defined boundaries, self-monitoring, accountability to third parties, and the close proximity of other people where mentorship meetings are held. This can be applied differently in diverse cultural contexts. However, we should not allow these measures to become a distraction. I would say that the most important factors for a good mentorship outcome, in any case, are these: the mentor and mentee must maintain a focus on the learning objectives of the mentoring relationship and be sensitive to the promptings of the Holy Spirit.

THE ISSUE OF POWER IN A MENTORING RELATIONSHIP

We have spoken briefly about power in the mentoring relationship in Chapter Seven, and I would like to discuss it further. This issue appears from time to time in some church traditions and cultural backgrounds.

Power Distance

People who study cultures have used the term "power distance" to define the distribution of power or variances in understanding power in relationships of different cultures.[121] They seek to describe hierarchal relationships between different members of a society. For instance, as a Canadian, I have a preference for an egalitarian approach to mentoring relationships. This suggests that I am part of a low power distance culture. However, this may not be the case in other cultures in which the power distance is much greater between those having authority (teachers, mentors, pastors) and those under their authority (students, mentees, parishioners).

A lesser or greater power distance is not necessarily good or bad. It's simply a way to describe different cultural realities. However, one of the impacts that a high power distance might have on a mentoring relationship is that the mentor will tend to take the initiative in setting the mentoring agenda and the mentee will be less inclined to express their learning needs.

In some cultural backgrounds, power distance may be inherent in the social structures. For instance, people coming from a higher social or economic standing may have a greater power distance from those perceived to be from a lower social standing. Ministry mentoring relationships need to be navigated carefully in such contexts. Both Jesus and Paul often set aside social conventions and were able to relate to people of all social classes.[122]

However, as people of one culture interact with those of another, cultural assimilation is likely to occur. They adapt their practices and change their behaviours in a way that reflects the influence that the other culture has on them. This is evident in the area of power distance and how it is perceived between a mentor and mentee. For instance, a mentee may have received training in a context where the power distance between the teachers and students was minimal, but then he begins a mentoring relationship with a pastor who has a more traditional understanding of power distance. The mentee may want to relate to his mentor with more familiarity than the mentor feels is appropriate. Or the mentee may come from a traditional background where deference is paid to superiors, so they don't feel

---

121 Geert H. Hofstede, Gert Jan Hofstede, and Michael Minkov, *Cultures and Organizations: Software of the Mind: Intercultural Cooperation and Its Importance for Survival*, third edition (New York, NY: McGraw-Hill, 2010), 53–88.

122 Jesus associated with the poor and marginalized as much as with the rich and powerful. The apostle Paul's mentoring of his spiritual son, the runaway slave Onesimus, is an example of breaking down of class barriers (Philemon 1).

comfortable when a mentor relates to them in an egalitarian manner. Either way, there may be a learning curve for both mentor and mentee as the relationship develops. Eventually, if they recognize what the issue is, they should be able to work it out.

This can also hold true when people from different cultures establish mentoring relationships. In a healthy mentoring relationship, we can expect to see a change in the relationship that reduces the power distance. Even Jesus' relationship with his disciples transitioned from servanthood to friendship.

Potential for Abuse of Power

Beyond the matter of power distance, there is also the matter of abuse of power. Whatever the power distance might be, as Christians we maintain that abuse of power in a mentoring relationship is wrong and misguided. There are nonetheless examples of such abuse in the history of the church.

The shepherding movement of the 1970s and 1980s is one example, because ministry mentoring and discipleship was a prominent feature of the movement. The shepherding movement, which also expressed itself in the form of a house church structure, had a rather controversial understanding of authority and governance. They placed a strong emphasis on submission, not just related to church matters but to all life matters. Marriage and career decisions were brought into the discipleship and mentoring relationship. S. David Moore, in his book *Shepherding Movement*, describes and evaluates this dynamic from a historical perspective:

> While freedom of conscience was always taught, followers knew that obedience to one's pastor was very important. Followers were not encouraged to an unquestioning, blind obedience to their shepherd but to an informal trusting obedience that was an outflow of a close caring relationship. The exercise of spiritual authority was well intentioned and seen as a means to bring health and maturity to people. Still, the emphasis on hierarchically oriented submission to God's delegated authorities led to

many cases of improper control and abusive authority throughout the movement.[123]

He further comments:

> The movement's leaders failed to recognize the downside of an authoritarian approach. Many of the young people joining the movement had not been adequately parented and were looking for an authority figure to fill their need. The movement leaders did not understand the codependent dynamic in many people. Further, the dictum 'power corrupts and absolute power corrupts absolutely' proved true in many instances. Human carnality got the best of some leaders, who used their authority in self-serving ways without sufficient or timely redress....The movement's emphasis on authority, submission, and servanthood had a way of silencing dissent. The highly personal, hierarchical, pastoral relationships made it difficult to disagree and challenge one's pastor without appearing disloyal. This was never intended, but it was a practical reality which its leaders have readily acknowledged. As a consequence some problems were perpetuated much longer than necessary.[124]

Ministry mentors will do well to take note of the potential dangers in a mentoring relationship, particularly when the mentor is in a position of power. We must not underestimate the allure of power in sustained learner-oriented formation relationships. The matter of submission to authority needs to be carefully defined at every level in authority structures associated with mentoring relationships. The words of Jesus need to be prominently engraved on the hearts of mentors and firmly entrenched in the habits of their leadership styles:

---

123 S. David Moore, *Shepherding Movement* (London, UK: Continuum International Publishing, 2004), 182.
124 Ibid., 186–7.

> *You know that the rulers of the Gentiles lord it over them, and their great ones exercise authority over them. It shall not be so among you. But whoever would be great among you must be your servant, and whoever would be first among you must be your slave, even as the Son of Man came not to be served but to serve, and to give his life as a ransom for many.*
>
> —Matthew 20:25–28, ESV

BUILDING TRUST, TAKING RISKS

As mentioned, the mentoring relationship is one of mutual trust. But trust will always involve a measure of risk on both sides of the mentoring relationship. From the perspective of mentors, a major obstacle I have come across is the inability to trust mentees because of stories of their negative experiences.

For instance, at mentorship training seminars, people often ask, "What if I mentor someone up to the point that they believe they are capable of leading the church or ministry? And what if they then undermine my ministry, split the congregation, and start their own church?"

Each context where a question like this is raised has its own unique backstory, but in a general sense it is analogous to the story of Absalom undermining the throne of his father David (2 Samuel 15:1–6). Sometimes the expressed concern originates from the mentor's own insecurity, which he needs to address before entering into a mentoring relationship in which he may feel threatened.[125]

But there is good reason to raise such questions, because there are true stories of those who have tried to displace a ministry's existing leadership.

Mentors cannot always know the motives of their mentees, but the possibility of mixed motives should not stop mentors and ministry leaders from taking the risk of investing in emerging leaders. It didn't stop Jesus from including Judas, even though *"Jesus had known from the beginning which of them did not believe and who would betray him"* (John 6:64).

---

125 Saul felt threatened by David's popularity not because David had tried to usurp any authority, but because Saul felt insecure (1 Samuel 18:6–9).

Part of the purpose and challenge of mentoring is to help mentees transcend and grow beyond their wrong motives and attitudes. The risk of mentoring is that some mentees may continue to make bad choices. But even more mentees will benefit from mentoring relationships and as a result become effective partners in the advance of ministry in a positive and productive way.

Mentors should default to trusting the motives of the mentees or trust in divine providence, which has a hand in orchestrating such mentoring relationships. At the same time, they should remain aware of potential issues with which they may need to deal. Any risk can be mitigated by the mentor paying attention to the early warning signs of discontent and finding ways to engage the mentee and confront issues in creative ways.

From another perspective, I have come across mentees who had negative experiences in mentoring relationships where their trust was broken. They became aware of serious flaws in their mentors and found it difficult to trust them again. They have transferred this mistrust to all potential mentors and become cynical about mentoring relationships. This may come from unrealistic expectations that are unlikely to be met in any context, but it may also be warranted by the emotional or spiritual abuse they encountered at the hands of those they trusted. They are afraid to risk again.

It is important for us to find ways to rebuild trust on both sides of the mentoring equation. It is not within the scope of this book to deal with this issue in depth, but here are a few points that, if considered, will help to increase trust. These apply to both mentors and mentees.

- Stay engaged. Do not disengage too quickly.
- Own your faults. Apologize and make it right.
- Have an attitude of forgiveness. Give second chances.
- Do not assume that no else is trustworthy because one person broke your trust.
- Trust God in the relationship, even if the human element fails.

Sometimes trust cannot be rebuilt sufficiently for the mentoring relationship to continue, so it is best to conclude it. But mentors and mentees should not be afraid to take the risk with others.

As we pointed out earlier, Paul was disappointed with John Mark, but he tried again with Silas. Barnabas, on the other hand, took the risk and continued with Mark (Acts 15:37–40). Their ministry continued, as did their ministry mentoring, and the gospel of the kingdom continued to advance.

WHEN THE MENTORING RELATIONSHIP BREAKS DOWN

Sometimes mentoring relationships break down, and it's not always because trust is broken. It can be due to many other factors, such as incompatibility of personalities, scheduling issues, or matters that are external to the relationship. Johnson and Ridley suggest,

> Mentors should be open to the possibility that things can go wrong. Because of their inherent imperfections and those of their protégés, mentors need to be alert to situations and interactions that might undermine their relationships. If things go wrong, they must address the problems quickly and attempt to restore the relationship.[126]

The same points concerning rebuilding trust can be applied here, if that is part of the problem. The mentor needs to be honest with himself and the mentee about what is happening. The process needs to slow down to encourage thoughtful reflection on the best way forward.

1. The mentor and mentee each need to be able to express how they see the issues and identify the problem.
2. They can each suggest solutions to the problem.
3. They can come to an agreement about which solution should be tried first.
4. They should seek consultation from trusted colleagues.

---

126 Johnson and Ridley, 129.

5. Careful documentation can also be a help in moving toward a resolution.

Some problems, however, cannot be fixed, but care must be taken to minimize the damage. If the steps listed above have been tried and there does not seem to be a workable solution, the formal mentoring relationship should be concluded in as gracious a manner as possible. Both parties should take this as an opportunity to learn from the experience and remain open to future mentoring relationships.

QUESTIONS: FROM REFLECTION TO ACTION

1. What other challenges have you found in mentoring relationships that have not been mentioned in this book? How would you address them?
2. What has been your experience of the issue of power in mentoring relationships? How did you address it?
3. What do you think it means to trust God in a mentoring relationship even if trust is lacking between two individuals?
4. What challenges may emerging women ministry leaders face as they seek access to good mentoring relationships when most of the Christian leaders are men? How can these challenges be overcome?

CONCLUSION

I REMEMBER THE SEASON IN OUR LIVES WHEN MY WIFE AND I HAD TO DRIVE OUR children to all the places they needed to be. As parents, we were happy to do it most of the time. But there were some days when we wished we could be doing something else, especially when other responsibilities demanded our time. So when the kids came of age and wanted to learn how to drive, we happily invested the time to teach them—and we gladly suffered the fender benders.

When our daughter Marlies passed her driving test, it was a day of rejoicing. I will never forget the day when she said to me for the first time, "Dad, can I have the car keys? I need to take Phil and Rich into Vancouver for a youth meeting."

Without hesitation, I handed the keys to her.

Outwardly I tried to remain serious and composed. "Okay, just drive safely." But inside, I was doing fist pumps and shouting, *Yes!* I realized that I had now been liberated from my chauffeur duties. I had always wondered why my own father had been so eager to teach us how to drive. Now I understood.

In due course, our boys also learned to drive, and we soon had a team of willing drivers in our home. We still drove the car from time to time, but we were no longer the only ones able to do it. We were successful in transferring our driving skills to them so that they could share in the family's transportation responsibilities.

I want to leave you with three broader applications of mentoring relationships: team building, succession planning, and embedding a mentoring culture into a ministry organization. These brief descriptions are suggestive of how mentoring fits into the bigger picture of church ministry.

MENTORING AND TEAM BUILDING

Ministry mentoring can play a role in team-building. I like Alan Wright's succinct definition of teams: "Teams are small groups of people who share a common goal to achieve a specific result."[127] Ministry mentoring relationships, as well as ministry teams, exist for the purpose of advancing the kingdom of God. By mentoring, we can build team members who share the vision, values, mission, and the ministry load. They may not all have the same function, but they are linked together by the same purpose. The biblical metaphor of the body of Christ teaches this:

> *For just as each of us has one body with many members, and these members do not all have the same function, so in Christ we, though many, form one body, and each member belongs to all the others.*
> —Romans 12:4–5

Ministry mentoring plays the role of helping individual members of a team to identify and embrace their unique function so the purpose of the team is ultimately fulfilled. Jesus equipped his disciples in the same way. He now continues to do this by the Holy Spirit and through the ministry gifts.

> *And he gave the apostles, the prophets, the evangelists, the shepherds and teachers, to equip the saints for the work of ministry, for building up the body of Christ...*
> —Ephesians 4:11–12, ESV

---

127 Alan N. Wright, *Spiritual Dimensions of Team*, Kindle edition (St. Louis, MO: Chalice Press, 2010), location 172.

MENTORING AND SUCCESSION PLANNING

By mentoring, we can identify and train those who will carry the vision beyond our ministry tenure and lifetime. If you are in leadership of any kind, you are replaceable. It will happen in one way or another. It can happen by an election process, by an insurrection of some kind, by being burned out, by retirement, by an unexpected death, or as a carefully planned transition. How blessed are those leaders (and their charges) who have discerned the right time to initiate the process of succession! It begins in a culture of mentoring and leadership development.

Leaders need to have the mentoring skills and mentoring attitude we have outlined in this book, as well as a carefully laid out strategy for selecting their successor and transitioning to the new leader. The strategy, different in each ministry context, will be contingent on the governance model of the church or ministry organization.

But whatever the governance model, the first part of the strategy is to develop a pool of potential successors who have been trained and mentored in the ministry context.[128] They will be found among the members of the ministry teams. They will have demonstrated leadership and ministry skills as team and group leaders. They may be singled out for more intensive mentoring. A biblical example is the core group of Jesus' disciples: Peter, James, and John.

Another part of the succession strategy is to find ways to step aside, giving potential successors the opportunity to step up.

Let me continue to develop the analogy of teaching our children to drive. They would never learn to drive while I was behind the steering wheel. I had to let them take the wheel and drive, but during the learning process I sat right beside them and gave them step-by-step instructions. As time went on, I offered less and less instruction until they received their license. But even afterward, on rare occasions I still offered the occasional driving tip.

---

128 Naomi Dowdy, *Moving On and Moving Up: From Succession to Significance* (Lake Mary, FL: Creation House, 2010), 63.

In all areas of ministry, it is of paramount importance to align ourselves with God's purposes in everything we do. This is no less the case in the selection of successors. The early church modelled this attitude when they prayed concerning the selection of Judas' successor: *"Lord, you know everyone's heart. Show us which of these two you have chosen to take over this apostolic ministry, which Judas left to go where he belongs"* (Acts 1:24–25). Note that the candidates were from the pool of those who had accompanied the apostolic team in their journeys with Jesus.

Some leaders have found it difficult to separate themselves from their positions and places in ministry. They ask themselves, "If I step aside, what do I do?" One of my mentors, Naomi Dowdy, writes:

> Leadership transition and succession does not mean that you will not continue doing what you love. More likely than not, if you have discovered your gift, passion and anointing, you will be using that gift—but in a different expression or larger capacity.[129]

In any case, ministry mentoring will likely be a part of what you do. God knows we need more mentors.

TAKING STEPS TOWARD A MENTORING CULTURE

The ongoing success and health of any church or organization is contingent on the effectiveness of its leadership development programs. Whether the leaders are employed or volunteer, when they are mentored in-house they are better able to embody the shared values of the organization.

While it's of the utmost importance to understand the mentoring relationship as a standalone arrangement, and while this remains the heart of any corporate mentoring initiative, it is also necessary to explore what it would take to incorporate mentoring into an organizational structure. In this book, I have spoken primarily about the mentoring relationship between the mentor and mentee. Occasionally we have alluded to a third stakeholder in the mentoring relationship—namely, the organization.

---

129 Ibid., 128.

Conclusion • 159

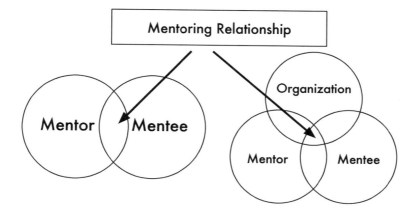

Figure 9: Mentoring Relationship Stakeholders

This adds another layer of structure and support to the mentoring relationship. This kind of initiative moves a church or organization toward creating a mentoring culture where there are enough mentors to skillfully mentor all those who require it. I don't recommend mentoring as another layer of administration or another program. I propose ministry mentoring as a culture that permeates everything within the organization.

How can this become a reality? What ingredients can make this possible where you serve in ministry? I invite you to consider the following steps, and as you do, envision how they can be adapted to your own context:

1. The leadership of an organization or church needs to embrace the value of ministry mentoring and understand how it relates to and supports all the other values of the church.
2. Imagine what your church would look like if every functioning ministry leader mentored at least one other person to be ready to take their place, or another place, in ministry.
3. Discover where ministry mentoring already exists in your organization, describe it, and ask how it can be strengthened.
4. Plan and provide infrastructure that includes the appointment of a mentoring champion who can coordinate mentoring initiatives throughout the organization.

5. Recruit and identify a pilot group of participants, both mentors and mentees. Identify mentee needs and mentors who are willing and able to engage them.
6. Set up a system to match mentors with mentees based on the existing culture of the organization.
7. Train mentors in the ministry mentoring principles outlined in this book, or a similar book. Also, train mentees on how they can make the most of a mentoring relationship.
8. Provide structural guidelines for the mentoring relationships. The guidelines in this book can be adapted to your context.
9. Monitor and evaluate the mentoring relationships. Find ways to measure the outcomes in ways helpful to your context.[130]
10. Bring others in the organization on board in successive cycles and watch your church become infused with a mentoring culture that no longer has a shortage of mentors. In addition, you will have a surplus of volunteers who are ready to serve anywhere.

As these steps are implemented, it is important to let your ministry context and culture determine the appropriate level of formal structures.[131] But remember: for any lasting change to take place, it will require a high level of commitment and intentionality.

---

130 Steps four through nine have been adapted from Allen, Finkelstein, and Poteet. Other suggested resources that discuss structured mentoring programs in organizations include Klasen and Clutterbuck, as well as Lois J. Zachary, *Creating a Mentoring Culture: The Organization's Guide*, first edition (San Francisco, CA: Jossey-Bass, 2005).

131 "The design of formal mentoring programs can vary considerably. Some programs are highly structured while others take a more casual approach. Research shows that programs with a greater degree of organizational facilitation and structure are generally more effective than those with little support and oversight... Notably facilitation and structure should not be equated with rigidity and inflexible formality. The form that the facilitation and structure takes needs to fit with the culture of the organization" (Allen, Finkelstein, and Poteet, 5).

ONE MORE THING

One day, I was reading the story of King Hezekiah. I couldn't help but be impressed at the strong commendation he received from the writer of the narrative:

> *Hezekiah trusted in the Lord, the God of Israel. There was no one like him among all the kings of Judah, either before him or after him. He held fast to the Lord and did not stop following him; he kept the commands the Lord had given Moses.*
> —2 Kings 18:5–6

He experienced divine intervention against the armies of Assyria, was miraculously healed from a fatal illness, and even observed a supernatural sign in which the sun reversed its course for a few hours.

I kept reading. He entertained guests from Babylon and gave them the royal tour, impressing them with the display of Judah's wealth. Isaiah rebuked him for this and then prophesied concerning the judgment that was coming to Judah, albeit not in Hezekiah's lifetime. I had read this many times previously. But this time, Hezekiah's response jumped out at me:

> *"The word of the Lord you have spoken is good," Hezekiah replied. For he thought, "Will there not be peace and security in my lifetime?"*
> —2 Kings 20:19

I was stunned, and asked myself, "What was Hezekiah thinking? Was he really okay with what was destined to happen to the next generation after him?"

Now, he may not have been able to change that destiny, because the die was cast long before his time. Perhaps he was aware of that. He had experienced the goodness of God and he was faithful in many ways that previous kings were not. But with that brief statement, he revealed something of his heart which troubled me. Why? It is also possible for us to become complacent concerning what happens after us.

A far better attitude was modelled by Samuel as he stepped aside from leadership to make room for the king:

> *As for me, far be it from me that I should sin against the Lord by failing to pray for you. And I will teach you the way that is good and right.*
> —1 Samuel 12:23

And he continued to mentor Saul, and later David, until he died.

★ ★ ★

A few months ago, I was in the back seat of the car where my daughter was teaching our oldest grandson how to drive. He was in the driver's seat and she was giving him instructions. He was now an emerging fourth generation driver. It is my prayer that his generation will also have ministry mentors who will transfer to them a living faith in the Lord Jesus Christ and Spirit-empowered ministry. I am confident that God will answer that prayer.

Appendix A

MENTORING AGENDA PROCESS WORKSHEET

Mentor Questions	Mentee Questions
How can I serve the mentee?	Who am I?
What is best for the kingdom of God?	What do I want to learn?
What mentoring skills do I need?	Am I willing to commit to the process?

MENTORING AWARENESS DISCOVERY QUESTIONS		
What was	**What is**	**What will be**
What is the story of the mentee?	How does the mentee understand their relationship to Jesus?	How do they want to grow in character?

What are the defining moments of the mentee's life?	What are the limitations and temptations the mentee is dealing with?	What ministry and life skills does the mentee want to learn?
Who are the significant people in the mentee's life?	What is the composition of the giftedness set of the mentee?	By what does the mentee want to be remembered?
Any other questions?	Any other questions?	Any other questions?

THE MENTORING AGENDA	
Character Development Agenda	**Competency Development Agenda**
Proceed to make THE MENTORING AGREEMENT	

Appendix B

SAMPLE MENTORING AGREEMENT

This is an agreement between <u>Tim B.</u> and <u>Cory M.</u>

We will meet regularly at these times: <u>once a week on Tuesdays at 10:00 a.m.</u>

Our means of connecting between meetings will be by <u>email or SMS.</u>

The Learning Objectives and Activities

A. Competency and Ministry Skills Learning Objective: <u>How to Lead a Small Group</u>

LEARNING ACTIVITY	WHEN
1. Study the small group leader's handbook.	Ongoing.
2. Observe the mentor as they lead.	Periodically.
3. Participate in planning with the small group's leadership team.	Whenever possible.
4. Practice leading small group discussions.	As requested.
5. Debrief on all of the above	Weekly, or whenever possible.
6.	
7.	

B. Character Development and Spiritual Formation
Learning Objective: _Anger Management_

LEARNING ACTIVITY	WHEN
1. Become self-aware by journaling and reflecting on times of anger.	Ongoing.
2. Study scriptures concerning anger and emotions.	Daily.
3. Discuss the insights you've gained with the help of the mentor.	Weekly.
4. Consider if other kinds of help are required.	As needed.
5.	
6.	
7.	

C. The short list of items which may be included in the mentoring agenda as learning objectives are:

• How to lead a prayer meeting.	• How to pray for the sick.
• How to evangelize.	
• How to have a regular devotional time with God.	

Duration of Agreement
- We will evaluate the mentoring relationship every _three months_.
- The intended length of the mentorship is _one year_, but it can be extended by mutual agreement.

Expectations:
- We have discussed the expectations of the mentor and the mentee. We have each taken note of each other's expectations and will review them after one month.

Confidentiality and Privacy

- Everything discussed in our time together will be kept confidential unless explicit permission is given to share a specific matter. We will respect each other's privacy and personal boundaries.

Signed: _____ (Mentor)

Signed: _____ (Mentee)

Date: _____

Appendix C

COMPONENTS OF THE MINISTRY MENTORING MODEL EXPANDED

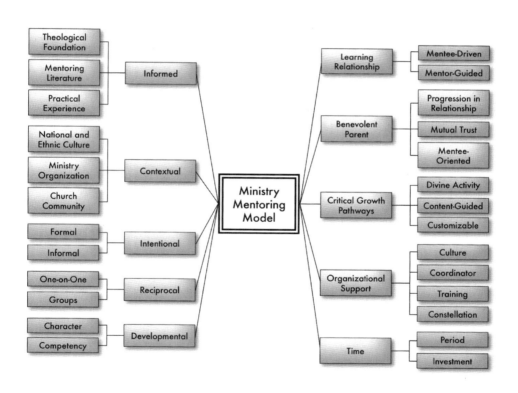

GLOSSARY

Coaching: a formational learning activity which focuses on the development of specific skills. The coach facilitates the learning of the person being coached by asking questions designed to help him or her achieve their learning objectives.

Critical growth pathways: the means by which the mentee moves toward fulfilling the learning objectives based on the mentoring agenda.

Competence: a person's general ability to do something successfully or efficiently (sometimes used interchangeably with competency).

Competency: a person's ability to perform a certain task; what a person brings to a job or ministry context that results in success (sometimes used interchangeably with competence).

Development plan: the specific program of learning activities that the mentor negotiates with the mentee.

Discipleship: as distinguished from ministry mentoring, it refers to the spiritual formation of a newly converted person. As part of ministry mentorship, it refers to a lifelong commitment to follow Jesus and submit to a learning process that leads toward spiritual maturity.

Enhanced informal mentoring: a mentoring relationship in which both the mentor and mentee acknowledge an ongoing arrangement without an explicit mentoring agreement.

Formal mentoring: a mentoring relationship which can be described as intentional, structured, controlled, and intensive. It usually includes a mentoring agreement.

Formational learning activity: any activity which adds to the learning of the mentee or the beneficiary of a learning relationship.

Giftedness set: The combination of natural abilities, acquired skills, and spiritual gifts.

Informal mentoring: mentoring which is organic, spontaneous, occasional, and relaxed. It may occur in the context of a relationship or as part of a brief mentoring encounter.

Intentional mentoring: where the mentor and mentee deliberately form a mentoring relationship that is sustained over time.

Mentee: the person being mentored, the main beneficiary in the mentoring relationship.

Mentor: the benefactor in mentoring relationships who makes his or her accrued knowledge, skills, wisdom, and experience available to a mentee.

Mentoring activity: a learning activity through which knowledge, skill, or wisdom is transferred to the mentee as a result of the mentor's involvement. In itself, a mentoring activity does not constitute a mentoring relationship.

Mentoring agenda: what the mentee wants to learn; the mentee's felt learning needs.

Mentoring relationship: a relationship between a mentor and mentee in which mentoring activities occur from time to time.

Ministry: means the same as service. The word *ministry* has taken on a vocational nuance in Christian circles, and it is used with that in mind in this book while intentionally retaining the tone of a serving attitude.

Ministry development: growth in the ministry skills which are required by a person in Christian ministry.

Power distance: the distribution of power or variances in understanding power in relationships. Low power distance cultures treat people of all ranks with similar respect while cultures with greater power distance ascribe different levels of respect depending on a person's perceived rank.

Spiritual formation: activities and disciplines which form the spiritual dimension of a person in such a way that it impacts his or her character development.

ACKNOWLEDGEMENTS

The writing of a book is a bigger project than I had imagined, certainly bigger than I am. I thank God for his sustaining power and for the many people with whom he has connected me on this journey. They deserve to be acknowledged for their direct or indirect contribution to this book. I will try to do this here.

I would like to thank the leadership of the Pentecostal Assemblies of Canada, who have created a large tent under which to serve the purposes of God both in Canada and around the globe. As a credential holder of that fellowship for all the years of my ministry, I thank God for the privilege of serving with the brothers and sisters of that tribe. And special thanks to the current General Superintendent, Rev. Dr. David R. Wells, for consenting to write the foreword to this book.

This book flows out of the thesis project which I did as part of the Doctor of Ministry program at Tyndale Seminary and University College, and I would like to acknowledge Dr. Paul Bramer and all the other professors and friends at Tyndale for their role in that part of the writing journey.

I thank the pastors and leaders of the Pentecostal Assemblies of Sri Lanka, who participated freely in the thesis project and were the first to be exposed to the earliest versions of what is now in this book. I also want to acknowledge subsequent mentorship seminar attendees, who by their questions helped give shape to the content.

I want to thank Dr. Naomi Dowdy, whose timely mentoring advice over the years ultimately led me to write this book. I also want to thank

John Caplin, who asked the kinds of questions that compelled me to complete the book.

Thanks to those who read portions of the manuscript and provided helpful feedback from different perspectives: Len, Jonathan, Valerie, Wes, Carli, Fred, Marlies, Phil, and Marilyn. And to Marty for help with the title.

I am indebted to many authors and researchers who have studied mentoring, and I have done my best to acknowledge them in the footnotes. I am also grateful to those not explicitly mentioned.

Thanks to the people at Word Alive Press, who worked hard to get the book into its final form: Sylvia St. Cyr, publishing consultant, who graciously managed the publishing project; Evan Braun, editor, whose writing experience fashioned the book into a much easier read; and others who worked behind the scenes.

I want to thank my mentors and mentees, who have not been mentioned by name here, but you will see evidence of their influence scattered throughout the book.

Thanks to the members of Bethel International Church, our home church, who explicitly supported this writing project with their prayers.

Thanks to Mom and Dad and other family members for their unceasing prayers and support.

I especially want to thank Elizabeth, my wife, who has been my chief encourager every step of the way on this writing project.

Any shortcomings in the book are my own.

ABOUT THE AUTHOR

Rainer Mittelstaedt began his pastoral ministry in Vernon, British Columbia in 1975. After two years, he and his wife Elizabeth were sent to Tanzania as global workers by the Pentecostal Assemblies of Canada (PAOC). Much of Rainer's ministry was focussed on teaching and training Christian leaders. He was also the principal of the Pentecostal Assemblies of God College in Mwanza, Tanzania for four years.

After returning to Canada, Rainer completed his Master of Christian Studies at Regent College in Vancouver. In 1988, he and his family went to Sri Lanka as global workers. Rainer established the Pentecostal Assemblies Bible College and was primarily involved in the training and mentoring of pastors and leaders.

In 1995, Rainer became the pastor of a multicultural church in Vancouver. He trained and mentored local church leadership for ministry in this cell-based church. During this season of ministry, Rainer also taught at Summit Pacific College as an adjunct instructor, served as a presbyter of the Vancouver section of the PAOC, and was on the leadership team of the Vancouver Pastors' Prayer Fellowship.

In 2007, Rainer and Elizabeth reconnected with the pastors, churches, and friends in their former ministry context in Sri Lanka. They travelled back and forth from Canada to Sri Lanka several times a year. They transitioned out of Canadian pastoral ministry by 2013 to become fully involved in Christian leadership development in Sri Lanka from their base in Canada. During this time, Rainer had completed his Doctor of Ministry degree in Leadership Studies at Tyndale Seminary and University College, graduating in May 2013. The focus of his thesis project was ministry mentoring in a Sri Lankan context. Based on the research of that study, Rainer has been developing a mentorship training course which he is teaching in various places.

In 2015, Rainer became the South-East Asia Regional Coordinator for Theological Education and Leadership Development for the PAOC International Missions and travels extensively in that region. He is currently developing a ministry mentorship training program for Christian leaders which includes the training and resourcing of other mentorship instructors. He is also promoting the integration of a mentorship training curriculum into Bible colleges and seminaries.

Rainer and Elizabeth currently reside in New Westminster, British Columbia. They are blessed with three married children who with their spouses and eight grandchildren give them much joy.

RECOMMENDED READING

Allen, Tammy D., Lisa M. Finkelstein, and Mark L. Poteet. *Designing Workplace Mentoring Programs: An Evidence-Based Approach*. Talent Management Essentials. Malden, MA: Wiley-Blackwell, 2009.

Brown, Steve A. *Leading Me: Eight Practices for a Christian Leader's Most Important Assignment*. Lagoon City, Brechin, ON: Castle Quay Books, 2015.

Clinton, J. Robert. *The Making of a Leader: Recognizing the Lessons and Stages of Leadership Development*. Revised edition. Colorado Springs, CO: NavPress, 2012.

Clinton, J. Robert, and Dr. Richard Clinton. *The Mentoring Handbook: Detailed Guidelines and Helps for Christian Mentors and Mentorees*. Altadena, CA: Barnabas Publishers, 1991.

———. *Unlocking Your Giftedness: What Leaders Need to Know to Develop Themselves and Others*. Pasadena, CA: Barnabas Publishers, 1993.

Coleman, Robert Emerson, and Roy J. Fish. *The Master Plan of Evangelism*. Thirtieth anniversary ed. Grand Rapids, MI: F.H. Revell, 1993.

Creps, Earl G. *Reverse Mentoring: How Young Leaders Can Transform the Church and Why We Should Let Them*. San Francisco, CA: Jossey-Bass, 2008.

Dowdy, Naomi. *Moving on and Moving Up: 10 Practical Principles for Getting to the Next Level*. Dallas, TX: Naomi Dowdy Ministries, 2006.

———. *Moving on and Moving Up: From Succession to Significance*. Lake Mary, FL: Creation House, 2010.

Engstrom, Theodore Wilhelm, and Norman B. Rohrer. *The Fine Art of Mentoring: Passing on to Others What God Has Given You.* First edition. Brentwood, TN: Wolgemuth & Hyatt, 1989.

Hendricks, Howard G., and William Hendricks. *As Iron Sharpens Iron: Building Character in a Mentoring Relationship.* Chicago, IL: Moody Press, 1995.

Houston, James M. *The Disciple: Following the True Mentor.* Soul's Longing Series, Volume Five. Colorado Springs, CO: David C. Cook, 2007.

Johnson, W. Brad, and Charles R. Ridley. *The Elements of Mentoring.* Revised edition. New York, NY: Palgrave Macmillan, 2008.

Klasen, Nadine, and David Clutterbuck. *Implementing Mentoring Schemes: A Practical Guide to Successful Programs.* Oxford, UK: Butterworth-Heinemann, 2002.

Pue, Carson. *Mentoring Leaders: Wisdom for Developing Character, Calling, and Competency.* Grand Rapids, MI: Baker Books, 2005.

Reese, Randy D., and Robert Loane. *Deep Mentoring: Guiding Others on Their Leadership Journey.* Downers Grove, IL: IVP Books, 2012.

Saccone, Steve, and Cheri Saccone. *Protégé: Developing Your Next Generation of Church Leaders.* Downers Grove, IL: IVP Books, 2012.

Smither, Edward L. *Augustine as Mentor: A Model for Preparing Spiritual Leaders.* Kindle edition. Nashville, TN: B&H Academic, 2008.

Stanley, Paul D., and J. Robert Clinton. *Connecting: The Mentoring Relationships You Need to Succeed in Life.* Colorado Springs, CO: NavPress, 1992.

Wright, Walter C., Jr. *Mentoring: The Promise of Relational Leadership.* Waynesboro, GA: Paternoster, 2004.

———. *The Third Third of Life: Preparing for Your Future.* Kindle edition. Downers Grove, IL: IVP Books, 2012.

Zachary, Lois J. *Creating a Mentoring Culture: The Organization's Guide.* First edition. San Francisco, CA: Jossey-Bass, 2005.

———. *The Mentor's Guide: Facilitating Effective Learning Relationships.* Kindle edition, second edition. San Francisco, CA: Jossey-Bass, 2012.

Zachary, Lois J., and Lory A. Fischler. *The Mentee's Guide: Making Mentoring Work for You.* The Jossey-Bass Higher and Adult Education Series. First edition. San Francisco, CA: Jossey-Bass, 2009.

Please visit www.ministeringforward.com for additional information and resources relating to the book.

To contact the author please send an email to ministeringforward@gmail.com